A Sense of Belonging to Scotland: The Complete Collection

First published in 2007 by Mercat Press
Mercat Press is an imprint of Birlinn Ltd,
West Newington House, 10 Newington Road, Edinburgh EH9 1QS

www.mercatpress.com

ISBN 13: 978-1-84183-107-7

Printed and bound in Slovenia by arrangement with Associated Agencies Ltd, Oxford

A Sense of Belonging to Scotland:
The Complete Collection

The favourite places of Scottish personalities

ANDY HALL

*'I always knew, even as a small boy, that I would leave
Scotland and travel the world. I always knew I would, in one
sense, never leave completely.'*
Gavin Esler, writing about Gairloch, Wester Ross

MERCAT

Contents

Foreword

'The rose of all the world is not for me.
I want for my part
Only the little white rose of Scotland
That smells sharp and sweet—and breaks the heart.'

The sentiments contained in this perfect poem, 'The Little White Rose' by Hugh MacDiarmid, have been my motivation for photographing the images in *A Sense of Belonging to Scotland*.

These special places have been chosen by well-known Scottish personalities from many different fields. My privilege and challenge as a photographer has been to see these locations through their eyes and to distil their feelings of belonging to that place in a single image.

Over a period of six years, I have travelled 30,000 miles, regularly making multiple trips to the same place, in search of the perfect light to capture the decisive moments when all the elements of light, composition, colour and texture came together in perfect harmony, often only for a fleeting moment. In trying to explore the often indefinable feelings of longing for and belonging to Scotland, my own love of the country has deepened and strengthened immeasurably.

Whether you are a native Scot or an adopted friend of Scotland, I would encourage anyone who has enjoyed these photographs and descriptions to think of your own place, whether it is chosen as a scene from childhood, a memory of breathtaking beauty or a location where you feel rooted to Scotland, and to visit it from time to time, even if it is only in your imagination.

It will refresh your soul.

Andy Hall
October 2007

Acknowledgements

In the course of producing *A Sense of Belonging to Scotland*, I've received much help from a variety of sources too numerous to mention but, in particular, my grateful thanks go to all of the participants in the book. They are all very busy people but, without exception, they have embraced the idea with enthusiasm and commitment.

I owe a huge debt of gratitude to Visit Scotland, particularly Philip Riddle and Karin Finlay, for recognising the uniqueness of this piece of work and giving me support and encouragement at critical times in its realisation.

I would like to thank Raeburn Christie, Clark and Wallace (solicitors) of Aberdeen and my good friend Keith Allan for their continued faith in my photography, which they have expressed in the form of financial support since my adventures in publishing began.

I am indebted to Niall and Jacqueline Irvine of Perspectives for the exceptional quality of their scanning work and their invaluable creative advice and to John Hutchinson of Still Digital for my black and white portrait scans.

I would like to acknowledge the role of my friends at Mercat Press, in particular Seán Costello, whose insight and enthusiasm has brought my dream to reality.

I'm grateful to the Royal and Ancient Golf Club of St Andrews, Cruden Bay Golf Club, Loch Lomond Golf Club, Gleneagles Hotel, Braid Hills Golf Club and Silverknowes Golf Club for permission to take photographs from their courses. Also Rangers Football Club for permission to include Ibrox; Historic Scotland and the National Trust for Scotland for permission to photograph Edinburgh Castle, Callanish in Lewis, Bothwell Castle, and Culzean Castle; and to Ardverikie Estate in Loch Laggan for giving me access to take Dawn Steele's photograph; and to Stirling Council for the Wallace Monument; to Glasgow City Council for permission to photograph from Kelvingrove Park for Eddi Reader's place of Kelvingrove Art Gallery & Museum.

I would particularly like to thank Ewan McGregor for valuing and unhesitatingly endorsing the quality of my photography and to Carol and Jim McGregor who have facilitated communications with Ewan since the first letter eight years ago. Your friendship and encouragement have meant a great deal to me and inspired me to achieve something of which we can all be proud.

My final love and thanks go to my wife, Sylvia, for her continued support and artistic insight.

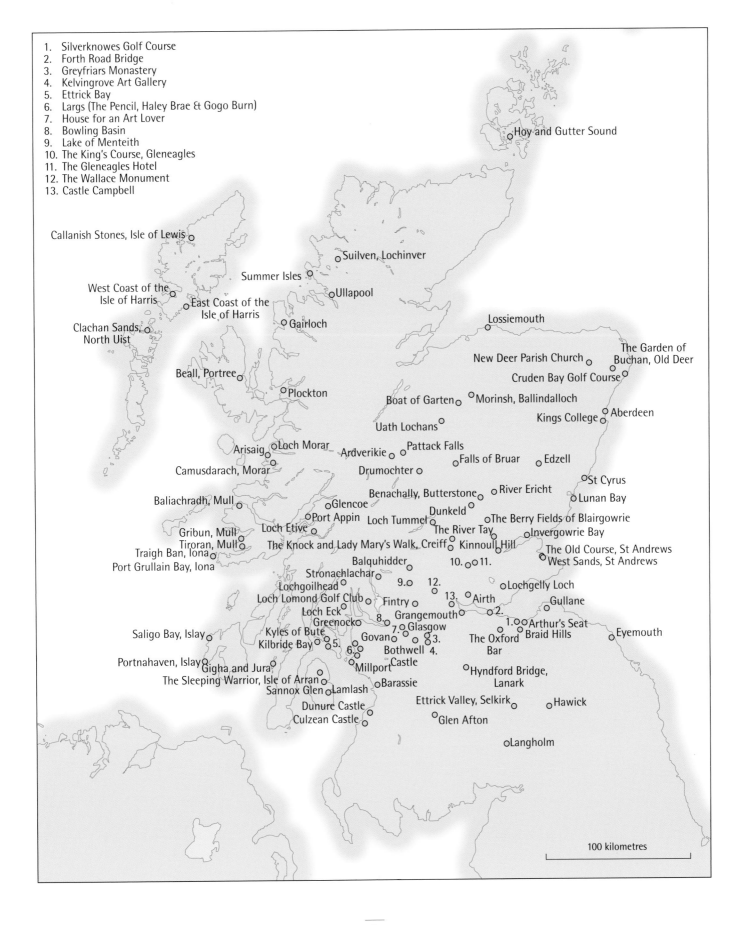

1. Silverknowes Golf Course
2. Forth Road Bridge
3. Greyfriars Monastery
4. Kelvingrove Art Gallery
5. Ettrick Bay
6. Largs (The Pencil, Haley Brae & Gogo Burn)
7. House for an Art Lover
8. Bowling Basin
9. Lake of Menteith
10. The King's Course, Gleneagles
11. The Gleneagles Hotel
12. The Wallace Monument
13. Castle Campbell

Hoy and Gutter Sound

Callanish Stones, Isle of Lewis

Suilven, Lochinver

Summer Isles

West Coast of the
Isle of Harris

East Coast of the
Isle of Harris

Ullapool

Clachan Sands,
North Uist

Gairloch

Lossiemouth

New Deer Parish Church

The Garden of
Buchan, Old Deer

Cruden Bay Golf Course

Beall, Portree

Plockton

Boat of Garten

Morinsh, Ballindalloch

Kings College

Aberdeen

Uath Lochans

Arisaig

Loch Morar

Ardverikie

Pattack Falls

Falls of Bruar

Edzell

Camusdarach, Morar

Drumochter

St Cyrus

Baliachradh, Mull

Benachally, Butterstone

River Ericht

Lunan Bay

Glencoe

Dunkeld

Port Appin

Loch Tummel

The Berry Fields of Blairgowrie

Gribun, Mull

Loch Etive

The River Tay

Invergowrie Bay

Tiroran, Mull

The Knock and Lady Mary's Walk, Creiff

Kinnoull Hill

The Old Course, St Andrews

Traigh Ban, Iona

West Sands, St Andrews

Port Grullain Bay, Iona

Balquhidder

10. 11.

Stronachlachar

9. 12.

Lochgelly Loch

Lochgoilhead

13. Airth

Gullane

Loch Lomond Golf Club

Fintry

Loch Eck

Grangemouth

2.

Greenock

8.

Glasgow

1.

Arthur's Seat

Saligo Bay, Islay

7.

Govan

3.

Braid Hills

Kyles of Bute

Bothwell

The Oxford
Bar

Kilbride Bay

5.

6.

Castle

4.

Eyemouth

Portnahaven, Islay

Millport

Hyndford Bridge,
Lanark

Gigha and Jura

The Sleeping Warrior, Isle of Arran

Barassie

Sannox Glen

Lamlash

Ettrick Valley, Selkirk

Hawick

Dunure Castle

Culzean Castle

Glen Afton

Langholm

100 kilometres

The Knock, Crieff, Perthshire

The favourite place of Ewan McGregor

The Knock in Crieff is a very special place to me. It reminds me of childhood holidays, of freedom and getting up to no good! I especially like this view looking over to Comrie from the indicator.

This particular picture has an almost three-dimensional effect. I really like the shiny film stock used. Many thanks for taking it and giving me a permanent, visual reminder of home.

The photographs in this book will inspire the beautiful melancholia experienced by Scots away from home all over the world.

Glencoe, Argyllshire

The favourite place of Ally McCoist

Glencoe is my favourite place, because, as you can see from the picture, time has no relevance.

Lunan Bay, Angus

The favourite place of Ricky Ross

I can't remember the first time I went to Lunan Bay but I do recall being there at many points in my life.

My friends in Primary 7 said I should join the Crusaders, as they were going camping there under canvas. It was this camp I remember best. We ate out in the open air, combed the beach, then straddled the nets to catch the wild salmon, and played a 'wide game'. The last event seemed to me to be the best organised fun I'd ever had.

All the time we drifted between the campsite, the sand dunes and the beach. I returned home having had one of the best weekends of my life. My mum enquired whether the recent downpours hadn't cast a slight shadow over the proceedings. I told her that the rain had been negligible as she emptied out my rucksack to find every item soaking wet.

I've been back since a few times. Sometimes with groups, but lastly with my own children. We jumped the same sand dunes and rejoiced in having this most beautiful place all to ourselves.

Andy's photograph does what all good photographs should do—catch the subject off guard. In the dead of winter, snow-covered, more beautiful than anyone could possibly expect, with only a few lonely footsteps to betray a solitary visitor.

People talk endlessly of Scotland's west coast—rightly so—but this stunning image shows the serene, low beauty of the east.

Loch Eck, Cowal

The favourite place of Emma Thompson

I saw Loch Eck for the first time when I was three months old. Since then, I've played on its banks, picnicked on its beaches, swum in its chilly, unsalted depths, cycled round it, drunk it, got drunk near it, kissed in boats on it, seen it change from blue to green to wizened old grey to frozen and stiller than death, made a film by it, got married near it and never wearied of it.

It is, in short, part of my DNA and I cannot do without it.

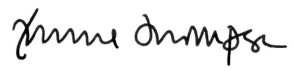

Govan, Glasgow

The favourite place of Sir Alex Ferguson

Looking at the photograph of the shipyard cranes invading the skyline evokes wonderful memories. Look how serene the picture is, and then think back and you realise that the very heartbeat of the Clyde is missing—the ships.

I can't believe what time has done to that great environment of noise, bustle and friendship. The caulker's hammer, the welder's flash, where has it all gone? And where is the Govan Ferry, where I was able to catch that incredible atmosphere of the shipbuilding era?

This picture represents the ghost of the Clyde, and yet a wonderful image of its past. When I look at it I can't help but feel the sadness and also the pride of being one of its sons. Long live the memory!

Alex Ferguson

The Oxford Bar, Edinburgh

The favourite place of Ian Rankin

To me, the Oxford Bar is an oasis. When I see that old, battered sign, I know I'm near friends and kindred spirits. The sign represents an old, unchanging Edinburgh, a tradition of friendship and storytelling.

Also, to me, the Oxford Bar represents another aspect of the hidden city. It's a minute's walk from Princes Street, but is hard to find. It's a 'well-kent secret', like the city itself.

Ian Rankin

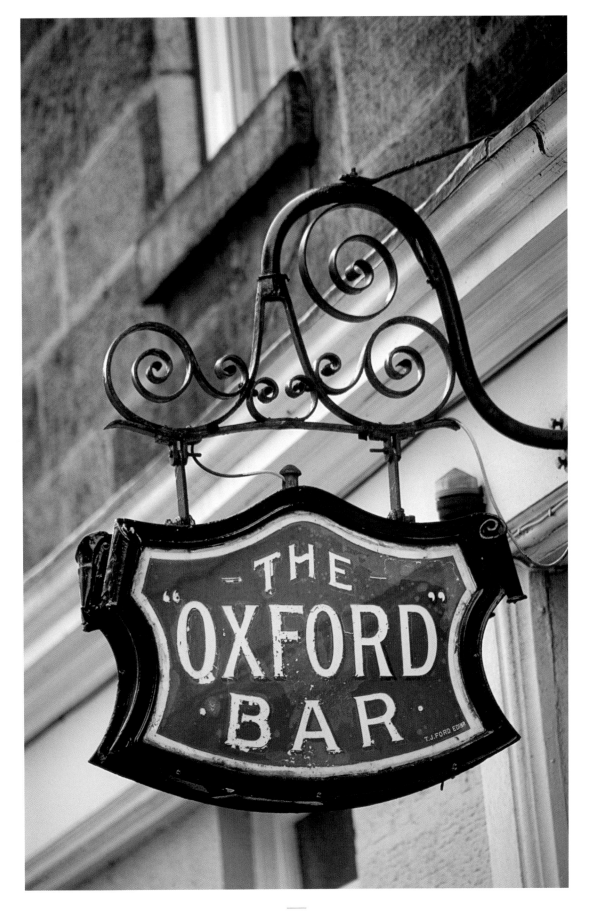

Saligo Bay, Isle of Islay

The favourite place of Lord George Robertson of Port Ellen

The island of Islay is unique. Its trademark whiskies, nature, scenery, and rich history make it stand out among Scotland's greatest national places.

But among its greatest strengths is its light. There is a distinctive purity and clearness of light, in all Islay's varied weathers, which I have seen in very few places in the world. This is especially so at Saligo Bay on Islay's north-west coast. This photograph captures a hint of what that brilliant, illuminating light does.

As a child, born on the island, we were regularly attracted to the magic of Saligo, and every trip produced excitement. Amid the rocks, the endlessly reshaped expanse of sand, the water in pools and the might of the ocean, we had the playground of dreams.

Then it became the favourite day out of our own children well into adolescence, and now a new generation knows the buzz.

A child, however perceptive, will not notice the light or recognise the fine and delicate beauty it imparts to a magnificent photograph such as this. But they know the place is special and different, and eventually they recognise that light and life are intimately connected, and therein is one of the secrets of the enduring vitality of Saligo Bay.

Pattack Falls, Strathmashie, Badenoch

The favourite place of Phil Cunningham

I stumbled upon this magical place on my first ever venture into the Highlands. On board the band bus and not expecting a scenic encounter, I found myself in a lay-by following a call for a 'rest' stop.

Whilst waiting for the others, I took a wander and had my first meeting with highland waters. It was one of the very rare occasions in my life where I was left speechless.

It still defies my ken, how something so dark and powerful can instil in me such a sense of peace, tranquillity and wonder. Since that day, I visit every time I'm near.

The ever-changing light ensures that it never looks the same twice, but it never fails to evoke that unforgettable feeling that started my love affair with the Highlands.

Andy has managed to capture the very essence of what I saw that day in this beautiful shot. That unique light, immense power and serenity... all rolled into one.

Tiroran, Isle of Mull

The favourite place of Andy Hall

Throughout the making of *A Sense of Belonging*, I have been asked about my own favourite place. Although I love Perthshire in autumn, Dunnottar Castle near my home town of Stonehaven and the mountains of the west coast in winter, I would say that Tiroran (the Land of Oran) on the Isle of Mull is the place for which I have a special affection. It was here that my mother was born in 1918 on an estate by the shores of Loch Scridain. More than anywhere else, it is here that I feel a sense of belonging.

When I look over the rocks, I can see my mother as a little girl playing in the rock pools with her sisters, Cathy and Bessie. Their home, America House (Tigh Ameireagaidh), was just yards from the sea, and as children they spent most of their time on the black, volcanic shores of the loch. The house itself had been transported from America and used originally as a community hall before becoming my mother's family home.

The girls loved combing every inch of the shore. Every Atlantic tide brought something new for them to play with. They decorated the rock ledges with bits of glass and china or anything that was colourful. No matter that the incoming tide washed down the shelves, they built them up again the next day.

One of my most treasured possessions is an account of their childhood written by my Aunt Cathy who stays near Bunessan on the way to the Iona Ferry. It is a very evocative description of the Tiroran of their childhood, not only of the people but also of the sights, sounds, smells and textures which seemed so abundant in their early years.

With a wonderful use of language that my mother also shared, she describes the carefree fun that they all had: the storytelling; walking to and from school in Scobul; watching out for fairies and snakes; the wild gentians, campanulas and the masses of white orchid by the wayside. She tells of their visits to Iona in a small open boat, soaked in seaspray and standing on the tiny island's hallowed ground with voices toned down to a whisper. I have visited Iona several times and can identify with that childhood experience.

My mother loved Mull, its landscape and its people. Despite moving to Perthshire in 1937, she held it always in her imagination. It is a beautiful island.

Andy Hall

The Summer Isles, Achiltibuie, Wester Ross

The favourite place of Evelyn Glennie

The sheer desolation of this community of islands that form the Summer Isles stretches all my senses in ways that no other place can.

Each island is a gem, so full of life in the minutest but most precious way. They embrace the seasons that transform them into a kaleidoscope of colour, moods, texture and richness. The only predictable aspect is that nothing stays still, as seconds, minutes and hours transform the very way these islands breathe.

I'm completely transformed as I witness the ingredients of nature and its expansiveness as it tugs at the very heart of my being.

Evelyn Glennie

Kelvingrove Art Gallery & Museum, Glasgow

The favourite place of Eddi Reader

When I fancied myself as a famous but troubled artist during my teens, I would spend every weekend up at the Kelvin Galleries sketching the 'Fishermen's Wives', gazing for hours at 'The Crucifixion' by Dali... or desperately looking for clues in the exhibitions of ancient ballroom gowns fully displayed with their gloves and little dance books.

I would be totally lost in the pencilled-in names on the books (obviously a queuing system for the blokes to dance with whoever was wearing the gown), which provided many hours of fantasy for me. It opened up all my creativity being exposed to all that. Thank you, Kelvin Galleries.

Eddi Reader x

The Forth Rail Bridge

The favourite place of Iain Banks

The Forth Bridge must have had an effect on me. I grew up with it outside my bedroom window and I moved back to the same village a few years ago, so I still see it every day.

All mile and a quarter of it is floodlit now, so it even looks enormously impressive at night too. I love its distant grace, its close-up massiveness, the colour of its hollow red bones against the stark clarity of a blue summer sky and its veiled bulk sieving the mists and clouds swirling above the winter river.

Iain Banks

Culzean Castle, Ayrshire

The favourite place of Colin Montgomerie

I spent my early childhood years growing up in Troon in Ayrshire on the west coast of Scotland. I returned to live there a few years later when my family moved back to the town and Troon was where I began the first steps of my career as a professional golfer.

This part of Scotland and the surrounding area have great memories for me and I feel immensely proud to have such close ties to this particular region.

Culzean Castle, a fine Georgian masterpiece by Robert Adam, characterises this region of Scotland for me and reminds me so much of where I spent my youth. The Castle stands high on a cliff midway between Troon and Turnberry Golf Clubs which, to me, are two of the finest links courses in Scotland and places where I played so much of my amateur golf, sometimes competitively and many times simply for pure pleasure.

The views from Culzean Castle are tremendous and from the Castle grounds it is possible to look out towards the mountains on the Isle of Arran. Andy's photograph captures the dramatic look of Culzean Castle superbly and this is exactly how it would look in the morning light. With such a pure blue sky the views to the Isle of Arran on such a day would have been fantastic. It truly is a magnificent example of a Scottish treasure.

East Lothian from Gullane

The favourite place of Alexander McCall Smith

There are some places where clouds and light combine in a particularly pleasing way. Whenever I leave Gullane in East Lothian, heading back to Edinburgh, the sky seems to put on a marvellous display, and for a moment I am transported back, magically, to a time of my youth, when such light seemed all about me.

This is a landscape that makes me shiver.

Alexander McCall Smith

Kinnoull Hill, Perth

The favourite place of Brian Cox

I remember it was just before my eighth birthday and the beginning of the summer, my birthday being the first of June, and my sister had just been taken to Dundee Royal Infirmary to give birth to my nephew, David. I remember my dad, my mum and my brother-in-law Dave going to Kinnoull, climbing up past the Cistercian Monastery up to the Folly. It had intrigued me ever since I was a baby when I used to go to Glasgow by car and see this lonely keep standing sentinel over the Tay Valley. Of course I didn't know then that this was a folly and had been designed as a homage to the Rhine, I forget by whom now, but some Scottish laird.

I can still physically feel it so strongly that when my dad and I came up to Kinnoull, there was a very narrow ledge across to the Folly, which I was a little fearful of. My dad slung me on his back and, closing my eyes, he took me across the ledge to the Folly. There we sat, eating sandwich spread sandwiches with bits of cheddar cheese, and gazing at the Tay Valley. I remember that my father was wearing a sleeveless, fawn-coloured pullover, and I had these tweed shorts on which used to chafe my inner thighs. My dad was so transfixed by the view that we just sat there in wonderment. We were alone so I don't know what happened to the rest of the party. I remember a great sense of literally being above it all and my dad said to me: 'You'll never see a finer view in your life, Brian.' I think this was the last private moment my father and I ever spent together, because within a year he was dead. The feeling was one of festivity, because here he was with his youngest son and proud of the fact that a grandson had just been born to him.

Kinnoull is about texture, smell and intimacy. Whenever I see Kinnoull Hill from the Perth Road, it is 100% associated with my dad and I always feel that his spirit is there watching, waiting for me to come home. This photograph completely captures everything I feel about Kinnoull.

Andy, a million thanks. I am so thrilled with it.

Brian Cox

The Old Course, St Andrews

The favourite place of Hugh Dallas

Where else in the world could you capture so much drama, joy, disappointment, belief, disbelief, and then, within a few hours, enjoy the freedom to stroll and enjoy public access to one of the most famous sporting arenas in the world?

St Andrews, as everyone knows, is the home of golf, and the spectacle of the sport's most coveted prize being decided on that final day on that famous final hole is memorable, to say the least, for everyone.

I vividly remember Jack Nicklaus's famous victory in 1978, Seve Ballesteros punching the air in 1984 as he sank his final putt, a victorious Nick Faldo in 1990, and who will forget Constantino Rocca's 65-foot putt in 1995 to force a play-off with John Daly and, of course, Tiger Woods winning in 2000 with ease.

Last, but by no means least, was Arnold Palmer playing up the 18th for his last time ever and stopping to be pictured on this famous bridge over the Swilken Burn.

Bowling Basin, Dunbartonshire

The favourite place of Marti Pellow

As a child I would often visit Bowling Harbour with my father to watch the ships go up and down the Clyde. Looking at the names of the ships and where they came from, like Chile or Argentina, always made my imagination run wild, as if this little spot was the gateway to the rest of the world.

My father used to go there as a child to watch the men offload their cargo, and when it was potatoes he would pick up the loose ones, build a fire and cook them by the side of the Clyde. This image always brings a smile to my face, and today as a man, whenever I have some time, I like to visit Bowling Harbour and just think of family and loved ones. It always seems to give me a great sense of peace, especially when it is raining and windy.

I feel that this photograph captures Bowling Harbour perfectly. For me it's quite a sad picture: the Clyde is no longer famous for its shipbuilding and the skeleton ships represent this for me. There is also a great sense of serenity to the photograph.

Thank you, Andy.

The West Coast of the Isle of Harris

The favourite place of Calum Kennedy

As a young boy growing up in Oronsay on the Isle of Lewis, I was fortunate to have the space and freedom to run and play by the sea. I was ten years old when my parents arranged for me to go to primary school in Harris where I learned to speak English—at least English with a Harris accent!

I remember being amazed by the difference in the landscape there. I love Andy's photograph because it shows Harris in all its glory and transports me back to my childhood. The seashore, the light, the freedom. I had not a care in the world… so many happy memories.

Calum Kennedy

The Gleneagles Hotel Golf Courses, Perthshire

The favourite place of Stephen Hendry

Gleneagles is only a stone's throw from my home and during my leisure time I spend many a happy hour on the golf courses. Despite my world travels, Gleneagles still remains for me one of the most beautiful places on earth.

Gribun, Isle of Mull

The favourite place of John Lowrie Morrison

My favourite place on earth—
    Gribun, Isle of Mull.
    Gribun of the thousand-foot cliffs.
    Gribun of the shafts of light.
    Gribun of the folklore.
    Gribun of the eagles and sea eagles.
    Gribun is primeval. Dark foreboding rock—strong light and even stronger colour.
    A feeling of standing on the edge of the world!
    Andy has conveyed this contrast wonderfully well—darkness versus colour—which is what my paintings are about—an allegorical description of the human spirit, if you like!
    Gribun just makes me feel the touch of the creator—the light—the colour—the wind. My best experience of Gribun was in a January gale with the wind and snow roaring like all creation was heaving.

Edinburgh Castle at Night

The favourite place of Louise White

In my childhood Edinburgh meant nothing more to me than the zoo. In my twenties I loved the shops and, call me a late developer, but it has only been in my thirties that I have truly begun to appreciate Scotland's jewel.

In recent years I have had the opportunity to report for Scottish TV on events around the city, such as the opening of the Parliament and the annual festival in August. Every time I make the journey from my home in Glasgow I see it in a different light.

However this photograph of the castle by Andy means much more to me on a very personal level. Work commitments prevented my husband Geoff and me from celebrating our wedding anniversary last year. It was postponed until November and we marked the occasion by spending a weekend in Edinburgh.

Late on the Saturday night, after dining at a restaurant close to the castle, we walked up to the esplanade. Gone was the mayhem, the visitors, their cameras and the tour buses; we only had the chill breeze and the stars for company. For once, there was no deadline, no script to write, no one to interview, just the chance to enjoy the midnight views and absorb a moment in time that will stay with me for the rest of my life.

Grangemouth Refinery at Night, Stirlingshire

The favourite place of Kaye Adams

I know it must seem like a peculiar choice to many people, but Grangemouth is not exactly overwhelmed with memorable architecture and the refinery gives it an unforgettable landmark.

When I was very young, I found it quite a scary place which I'd be nervous of approaching on foot or on my bike. When I was driven through it, however, it seemed strangely glamorous.

I have to say this photograph perfectly captures my favourite view of the refinery. It has a magical quality at night, particularly near Christmas time. I always used to think it was the finest display of fairy lights in the land.

Having said all that, we should be grateful you can't smell a photograph!

Kaye Adams

Loch Lomond Golf Club, 17th Green

The favourite place of Gordon Smith

I was thrilled to play Loch Lomond because of its reputation for being one of the world's most challenging courses set in one of Scotland's most beautiful locations. The walk was spectacular even if, at times, the golf was not.

However, I well remember the moment on the 17th green as I crouched to get a line on what was still a crucial putt. In an instant I had looked over beyond my ball and had taken in a view that was of stunning beauty and tranquillity. I was moved to stand up and invite my playing partners to enjoy the scene with me, which they duly did.

I don't believe that a moment like that can be captured in a still photograph but I have to compliment Andy on his beautiful shot which goes a long way to replicating my exact view of the Loch and surrounding hills. It's a marvellous photograph which encapsulates my 'moment' and evokes pleasant memories of a special day.

Gordon Smith

Port Grullain Bay, Isle of Iona

The favourite place of Kevin McKidd

When I was in my last year of primary school our class did a project on the island of Iona, culminating in a week-long school trip to the island. Being from Elgin in Moray, I had never been any further than Aberdeen or Inverness in my life.

This huge adventure to Iona had (and still has) a profound effect on me, never having been to the west coast. My childish eyes were struck by the beauty of it all. It seemed at once exotic compared to the rolling arable land of Moray, and strangely spiritual. Rambling around the bays and coves of the island, we were blessed with warm sunshine and endless days.

This particular spot on the west coast of the island became a favourite of mine. I remember picnicking on the grassy ledges of the ridge you see and falling asleep there to the sound of sea and gulls as a gentle summer breeze kept us cool. I vowed then that when I was a grown-up, I would return to this place.

Almost twenty years on I am (supposedly) now a grown-up and have returned to Iona many times. I have hitched there as a student and introduced its quiet charms to good friends over the years, all of whom seem to agree that it has a special quality that is hard to describe. I have camped (illegally) on the elevated machair to the right as you look at the photograph.

I took my wife to the island when she was eight months pregnant, as I suddenly had the urge to show her this place before we became parents. We walked around the north of the island, which is boggy and hard going at the best of times, let alone when carrying a small person inside you, but as we came over the ridge to see the Bay at the Back of the Ocean, she realised why we had come. We again picnicked on the grass, then fell asleep in the afternoon sunshine, the three of us.

Andy's photograph captures for me these happy endless summer days and makes me feel homesick for Scotland, but especially Iona. I am honoured to be part of this book and hopefully it will make a few others make the extra effort to reach this beautiful, remote spot. Thank you, Andy.

My next trip will be when my two children see this place. I can't wait and I hope they see as much in this small island as I do. They are called Joseph and Iona.

The Pencil, Largs, Ayrshire

The favourite place of Sam Torrance

They say that home is where the heart is. This is definitely where my heart is. I have been to many beautiful places around the world, but none please me more than this.

When I lived in Largs, this view from my bedroom window managed to have a different look every day. I could sit and look at it for hours on end. I hope you enjoy the view as much as I did.

Glen Afton, Ayrshire

The favourite place of Sir Tom Hunter

When Andy Hall asked me to name the place that resonated with me most in Scotland, I didn't hesitate—Glen Afton in Ayrshire. Many might say it's not the most beautiful of spots in Scotland, but to me it tells a huge story.

Growing up in New Cumnock, our lives were dominated by the coal mines, many of our families knew of nothing more. School for us then was claustrophobic, meant nothing to us and prepared us for one destination—yes, you guessed it—a career down the mines. The careers officer didn't have a tricky job!

So when me and my mates like Rab the Rhymer—still a great friend to this day—got off school we'd 'beat it' and march out to Glen Afton. It was space, freedom, opportunity and a chance to open our minds, to dream of what could be, rather than what would be. It opened our horizons, only for school to then close them for us.

To this day it reminds me of why I'm so passionate about Scottish education being fit for purpose, opening minds not closing them, and giving every kid an opportunity to shine—to be all they can be.

As for us, Rab headed to meet his pre-destined role down the mines and I went my own way thanks to my dad. Today, Rab is one of Scotland's best poets in my opinion—it took him twenty years to discover it. I wonder where he'd be now if our education had been a little different then?

Baliachradh, Isle of Mull

The favourite place of Sally Magnusson

I discovered Baliachradh when I was hunting for the township where my people came from on Mull. It was where my great-great-grandfather, James McKechnie, spent his early life, one of those sad and empty places you find all over Mull, relics of a lost community.

When I found it, I thought Baliachradh was one of the most enchanting places that I had ever seen. As the photograph suggests so translucently, it's not majestic, or breathtaking, or even wild and desolate in the way of Scotland's most striking landscapes, but rather touchingly domestic.

With its scattering of ruined stone houses arranged around kiln and grazing land, its once-neat vegetable patches, its shelter from the sea which glints just beyond the hill, Baliachradh felt overwhelmingly homely. It still feels a bit like home.

Arisaig, Lochaber

The favourite place of Gerry Rafferty

I first visited this part of Scotland with my mother, father and brothers when I was seven years of age. For the few days we were there, we were lucky because the weather was hot and sunny, which made the whole experience even more beautiful.

Andy has captured the wonderful quality of light which can be experienced in that part of the west coast of Scotland.

This particular view of Rum and Eigg from the mainland evokes so many magical childhood memories for me. And I am so pleased to have such a beautiful photograph of somewhere that is very dear to me.

So thank you, Andy. A wonderful piece of work and thanks for asking me to contribute. It was an honour.

Gerry Rafferty.

Loch Morar, Lochaber

The favourite place of Sir Cameron Mackintosh

I first went to the West Coast with my grandmother and aunts in the early 1950s when I was six. The idea of sleeping on a steam train had me wild with excitement from the moment I boarded the West Highland overnight express at London's King's Cross Station—a marvellously grimy and mysterious cathedral of a building, filled with the hubbub of bustling crowds and swirling steam. It was a great adventure to wake up in the early morning and be given a delicious bacon sandwich at Crianlarich Station, after which the train laboured over the stark, rugged beauty of Rannoch Moor, the line's highest point at over 1,000 feet. The rail journey then continued down to Fort William and along the 'Road to the Isles' to Mallaig. It is one of the most beautiful in the world and it has never failed to thrill me. Before one arrives in Mallaig, you pass the shimmering silvery sands of Morar, still mainly unspoiled and featuring spectacular views out to the Isles of Rum, Eigg and Skye. Here, with my bucket and spade, I dug sandcastles, collected shells, found a myriad of creatures under rocks and seaweed and beautiful driftwood shaped by the wind and stormy Atlantic seas. I thought it was paradise and though I now have had the luck to travel the world, it still remains virtually unchanged and is the most special place I have ever visited.

Over the years, I've got to know some of the mysteries that sandwich themselves between the hustle and bustle of the busy seaport of Mallaig. I've languished among the beautiful, almost tropical, islands that lie in Loch Morar, covered with fully-grown and untouched forest, left just as nature intended. Whatever the weather, the whole area has an extraordinary beauty; even when it's really wet, it's nice to be indoors by a nice fire with a dram and watch the weather rush by.

When the sun is shining (and it does much more than people think), then its unspoiled beauty is incomparable. Long known as a fabulous area to sail in, there are numerous idyllic spots to explore around the coast and nearby islands. My estate is bounded to the south by Loch Morar, which is the deepest inland freshwater lake in Europe, and to the north by the sea loch, Loch Nevis (which is Gaelic for Heaven), and has fantastic views over the Cuillin Mountains in Skye.

The sunsets on the West Coast are quite magnificent and this beautiful photograph gives just a taste of the magic of the place. Recently I travelled to Patagonia and when I got there, enjoyable as it was, I felt that the West Coast of Scotland was a lot more spectacular and varied and much easier to get to!

Silverknowes Golf Club, Edinburgh

The favourite place of Gordon Strachan

This is it! Young Strachan's world in the sixties, and I knew even then that this was a special view. Sitting on the steps of Silverknowes Golf Club on a warm summer's evening in the late sixties, trying to track my father's finish to his round of golf, was usually the end to a fun-packed day.

Hours of football with my mates or maybe a round of golf with the same lads; sometimes both were accomplished, always with the view of the Firth of Forth as the backdrop. I wondered where the big boats were going, where they had been and what they were carrying.

Today, when I sit here, I can still smell the grass stains on my jeans. I can still feel the warm breeze against my face, wondering if my dad will ever get a birdie four up the last.

Gordon Strachan

Beall, Portree, Isle of Skye

The favourite place of Donnie Munro

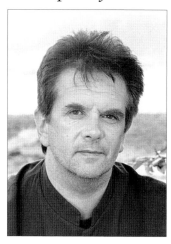

There are many places that we encounter on our travels which leave a deep and lasting impression on our minds. Amidst the excitement of the discovery of the new, it has always been important for me to return to that space where you feel utterly connected. A part, if you like, of something which simply is.

For me that place has always been Beall, just a short walk from my family home in Scorrybreac. Here the boulder-strewn landscape folds out onto the rolling green 'flats', running gently upwards to the high headland overlooking the Sound of Raasay and beyond to the hills of Wester Ross.

Here in the stillness of time is a settled feel, of all that has gone before, and a sense of scale that seems, at least for a moment, to make sense of all things.

Donnie Munro

Balquhidder and Loch Voil, the Trossachs

The favourite place of Hannah Gordon

The first time I visited Balquhidder was on a freezing, damp and foggy November day in 1987. I had come with my brother to view a cottage overlooking Loch Voil. It was virtually derelict, uninhabited for the previous five years, and badly in need of a new roof, a damp course, and much more. I couldn't wait to get my hands on it! About fourteen months later it was my pride and joy, and nothing will ever surpass the pleasure of bringing it to life.

Balquhidder is a well-known beauty spot and remains steadfastly unspoiled. It 'enjoys' a far above average rainfall, and one old lady, on hearing where my cottage was, remarked, 'Oh, aye, I know it well. Rain and midges!' But to me it is one of the most special places in Scotland. On a calm and sunlit day it takes your breath away; the loch like glass, the grandeur of the hills, the utter stillness and tranquillity. I have seen more stars here on a clear night than almost anywhere else, and marvelled at its beauty in winter…

I could go on, but I think by now you've got the message. Besides, Andy's photograph says it all.

Hannah Gordon

The Sleeping Warrior, Isle of Arran

The favourite place of Kirsty Wark

There's a point on the road from Lamlash to Brodick when you rise up the hill and get your first sight of the mountains and hills of Goatfell and the Sleeping Warrior. I look forward to that moment every time I make that journey. When the hills are snow-capped the view takes on another aspect—it could be the Himalayas!

This scene roots me to Scotland—I couldn't imagine not being able to see it. When it comes into view, I get a great sense of belonging.

Kirsty Wark

The Lake of Menteith, Stirlingshire

The favourite place of Nick Nairn

I grew up with this view, looking across the Lake of Menteith to Ben Lomond, and am lucky enough to enjoy it nearly every day of my life. It's never the same two days in a row. For instance today, as I write, the water is steely grey and Ben Lomond is invisible behind a curtain of mist, whereas Andy's picture is chocolate-box perfect. He took this picture in the summer, when we get the most spectacular sunsets—sometimes you can almost imagine Ben Lomond as an active volcano spewing lava across the horizon.

Having known this view all my life, it never fails to stimulate or soothe me. Somehow, and I can't explain this rationally, it helps define my Scottishness, it connects me to the landscape—especially the play between hills, water and light which, for me, are the essence of Scotland.

Nick Nairn

Aberdeen Harbour

The favourite place of Denis Law

I left Aberdeen when I was 15 to join Huddersfield FC. It was the first step on a career that would take me all over the world as a club player and as an internationalist. At that time, Huddersfield was an industrial town made up largely of cloth mills and was quite unlike Aberdeen, the Granite City, known mostly at that time for its thriving fishing industry.

My father was a fisherman and would sail out of this harbour for six days at a time, except when he went to the Faroe Islands, which was a three-week trip.

Whenever I return to Aberdeen, I visit Mike's fish and chip shop in Torry, make my way to Balnagask with my wife, Di, and enjoy the peace and quiet of this view over my home city. It is so close to the bustling harbour, always full of life, and yet it is almost like looking in from the outside.

A trip we often make from here is to drive down the coast to Stonehaven. I have many childhood memories of visits to the wonderful open-air pool in the summer, but these days, we always make for the picturesque harbour.

After a leisurely walk along the harbour front, we head over the Slug Road and visit the Falls of Feugh, just a few miles outside Banchory. The river can be spectacular after rain as it rushes through woodland and over rocks, particularly beautiful in autumn. We then complete our circular tour by driving back into Aberdeen along the South Deeside Road.

When Andy asked me to identify my favourite place in Scotland, I was undecided between Aberdeen Harbour from Balnagask and Stonehaven Harbour, but I opted eventually for this particular view because of its personal associations with my father and my deep affection for the city of my birth.

Andy has caught the atmosphere exactly as I keep picturing it. A perfect photograph that sums up everything that I remember about Aberdeen Harbour.

Denis Law

The River Ericht, Rattray, Perthshire

The favourite place of Fred MacAulay

I was privileged to grow up in Perthshire: Callander, Killin, Rattray and Scone. At both Killin and Rattray, the rivers Dochart and Ericht were significant in my surroundings and my upbringing. My parents still recall the time I pedalled my tricycle into the lade at the side of the Dochart when I was five years old.

But it is the Ericht that I remember more. It had claimed the life of one of the boys in my Cubs and maybe that gives it an extra air of mystery. I used to cross it on a daily basis and it was never the same twice. On the one hand, I've seen it so dry that you could have walked over the stones without getting your feet wet (not that I tried). And I've seen it in terrifying full spate after a period of sustained rainfall or in spring with the snows melting on the hills.

I don't know why, but my memory is of always crossing the bridge on the upstream side and staring at where all the water was coming from, just as you see in the photograph, rarely looking down to where the river flowed away. Maybe that says something about my character or my psyche. Or maybe it's because that's the side of the road our house was on!

Fred MacAulay

The Berry Fields of Blairgowrie, Perthshire

The favourite place of Stuart Cosgrove

So many of my early memories were forged on the berry fields of Perthshire. I was a member of the Letham Squad, a busload of pickers that would be taken from my housing scheme in the northern edges of Perth to the Essendy fields near Blairgowrie.

The Berries were a wonderland of words like luggie and dreel that had survived almost unchanged from Old Scots. You picked raspberries into a luggie which, by my time, was a plastic bucket, and to pick strawberries you were allocated a dreel, a row of berries that stretched up through the field. The object was to pick it clean, fill punnets to the brim, and then carry them to the weighing station where you were paid.

The Berries were a peasant experience turned working-class. Those that went were often from the poorest families in Perth and it was often very rowdy and hectic. The highlight was a piece break where you could gorge on rolls and Vimto. It was a very maternal environment, dominated by women and children.

Some of the most powerful images I have of self-confident femininity were forged at the Berries. The woman who hired the bus and led our squad was Mrs Soutar, mother of the famous Stagecoach millionaire, Brian Soutar. This was one of their first ventures into transport. When there was a dispute over wages, it was Mrs Speirs and Mrs Watt who led the delegation up to the Big Hoose to ask for another penny a pound.

As a kid with eczema, I probably should have been kept away from the Berries, and remember nights clawing away at my wrists. They were always red-raw with allergies. But when the bus arrived at night to take you home and you 'made' two quid, it was a great feeling of triumph over adversity. Sometimes we managed to steal a few punnets—hidden in the sleeves of an anorak—and then sell them outside Charlie's chippy back on the scheme.

The pickers are now drawn from Eastern Europe, especially the Czech Republic, and casting back further to the pre-war era, it was Irish labourers who came to pick Essendy clean.

What I most like about the Berries is the way it captures Scotland's changing social anthropology. I can't eat a strawberry now without memories flooding through my mind. It is a real sense of belonging, of being from a community that I still massively respect.

Eyemouth Harbour, Berwickshire

The favourite place of John Bellany

Eyemouth for me is one of the most beautiful places in the whole world. Beauty is a difficult word to define, but Eyemouth is beautiful.

The harbour which runs through the town is the hive of activity it always was, especially when all the boats come in from the fishing. The sights and sounds of the harbour area fill my heart with such rich memories of my past and the past in general. The history of the area, from the Eyemouth disaster and further back to the time of *The Bride of Lammermoor*, combined with the sheer stoicism of its people, fills me with an enormous sense of the continuum of life, with all its rich tapestry.

I have painted this home territory so often, sometimes drawing on childhood memories, sometimes on observation. Some of the allegories are from my fertile imagination, especially those of the Eyemouth disaster, which happened in the year my grandfather was born.

Eyemouth gives me a perpetual sense of wonder.

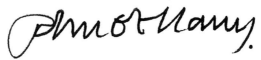

Stronachlachar, Loch Katrine, the Trossachs

The favourite place of Jimmie Macgregor

In the film Rob Roy, there is a dramatic scene in an old castle on a tangled island. The night is black and there are murky deeds afoot. A deadly confrontation takes place in which actor Brian Cox, who is very good at being a baddie, gets his comeuppance from an obvious goodie, a Macgregor. The baddie is one Graeme of Killearn, a nonentity raised to notoriety by dint of sheer nastiness. He was factor and general lickspittle to the heid baddie, the Duke of Montrose and, in the film, is knifed and drowned in the loch. No such event took place in reality, but Graeme did take a few knocks at the hands of one Rob Roy who had become a trifle miffed at Montrose.

The little island which lies off Stronachlachar (the Point of the Mason) on Loch Katrine is where the feckless factor was held to ransom by Macgregor. The Duke was deeply unimpressed and refused to pay up, and Rob Roy simply got fed up and let Graeme go, unknifed and undrowned. If you want to take a close look at what is now known as Factor's Isle, treat yourself to a superb trip to Stronachlachar from Trossachs pier aboard the perjink little steamer, the SS Sir Walter Scott. The island was originally named Eilean Darrach, or Oak Tree Island, and has been built up to protect it from the raised levels of Loch Katrine.

Jimmie Macgregor.

Suilven, Lochinver, Assynt

The favourite place of Dorothy Paul

I love Suilven because, when I was a girl, I had a cycling holiday up north and I remember going round a bend in a single-track road and being astounded to see this great mountain in all its glory.

I love the area in all its weathers and it surely can invite some rain and storm. Perhaps I am biased but I believe this is one of the most beautiful countries in the world. I say that, though, from my centrally-heated home. What must it have been like for the Picts!

Dorothy Paul

Bothwell Castle, Lanarkshire

The favourite place of Siobhan Redmond

Throughout my childhood and well into my adolescence, the Redmonds went on jaunts to Bothwell Castle. We held no truck with cars (or fashionable footwear), so the four of us, Mum, Dad, my sister Grainne and I would get the red bus to Uddingston and walk out from there.

Even getting the red bus made us feel quite holidayish—we spent large amounts of our city-bound lives on Corporation transport so a Lanarkshire bus was an almost exotic novelty.

The favourite time to go was early in the year when the snowdrops come out; later there'd be breathtaking displays of bluebells, but I always loved the tottie and tenacious snowdrops cocking a snook at winter.

What Andy's photograph captures so beautifully is the fairytale moment when this fun-size castle lies just before you—I love the domestic feel of the building and the approach through the wee winding wood.

I was an utter romantic (and a perfect pest) as a child, only occasionally emerging from my private pretend life as a princess. I distinctly remember singing 'Mary Queen Of Scots' Lament' from up in the tower and thrilling at the thought of her there in her love-struck days, all desperate and doomed. Oh, the glamour of it...

And on the way home there'd be Tunnock's tearooms with Jackie, their mynah bird, starring throughout as waitress: 'Pie and chips for two, Margaret!'; customer: 'Rangers for the cup!'; and advertisement: 'Tunnock's Caramel Wafers!' Then the exciting red bus back to Tollcross and the rare sensation for my bookish family of having had a day in the actual outdoors.

I'm so delighted to have this picture from my own long ago realised for me by Andy—it rushes me down the years to a time of treats and togetherness and the infinite promise of springs still to come.

Siobhán Redmond

The River Tay, Perthshire

The favourite place of Ken Bruce

As a teenager I spent several summers during the sixties in and around Aberfeldy, Kenmore and Pitlochry.

I cast my first fly, drank some of my first beer and had some of my best laughs amongst the hills of Perthshire. The peace, the stillness and the security of the surrounding hills are all strong memories to this day.

If there is a more beautiful sight than the Tay meandering through the Perthshire hills, I've yet to see it.

Ardverikie, Loch Laggan, Lochaber

The favourite place of Dawn Steele

When I first arrived at Ardverikie, this is the sight that hit me. The house itself has a driveway; not any normal driveway, though—a fifteen-minute car journey. It winds round the loch so, as you drive, you get the most amazing views.

This photograph of Ardverikie from the loch side means so much to me. It's hard to explain why, but it is so engraved on my memory because for seven months of the year (for five years!) it was the first thing I saw going to work and the last thing I saw on my way home.

A lot has happened on that beach, on and off camera! In the hot summers (yes, we did have a couple of days!) we had barbecues, swam in the loch (!) and sunbathed. While filming, we have had funerals, parties, deep family revelations, balls, highland gatherings—you name it!

We have filmed so many scenes here. Directors love it as it's such a fantastic backdrop. We used to feel a bit out of place in the scene, shoved to the side! I do miss it a lot. It's amazing when it's hot weather as you have this rugged Scottish countryside along with a bright white beach, but also mountains covered with snow! Although I've never been to New Zealand, I can imagine that this is maybe what it looks like.

This photograph means love, friendship, laughter and tears. Five years of it!

Benachally, Butterstone, Perthshire

The favourite place of Dougie MacLean

Above my house in Butterstone is a hill called Benachally. On top is a beautiful stone cairn. It looks out over Strathmore to the south and the Grampians to the north, two very distinctive landscapes. Over the years, I have spent a lot of time there with my family—grandparents, parents, uncles and my own children. It has been so often the place to aim for on picnics and walks with three generations of MacLeans. I have a photo of my mother as a young woman standing on top of the cairn.

The hill can be seen from some distance away, and on returning from long concert tours I knew that when Benachally came into view I was almost home! Andy Hall's beautiful photograph captures so well my feeling of affection for this very special place.

Boat of Garten Golf Club, Strathspey

The favourite place of Gavin Hastings

Boat of Garten Golf Club is certainly one of Scotland's 'Hidden Gems' and I would challenge anyone not to be inspired by the wonderful views and sheer beauty of the place.

Although it would be impossible to play golf when this photograph was shot, it does capture the peacefulness and clarity of this part of Scotland which makes playing golf here such a memorable experience.

It doesn't take long for any visitor to feel welcome and at home when you are this close to nature.

St Cyrus, Kincardineshire

The favourite place of Colin Prior

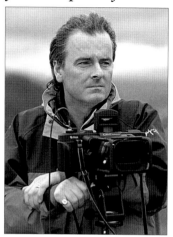

My favourite place is a difficult call. What sets St Cyrus apart from the others is the time I spent there as a child. We had a holiday home in Montrose and I was instinctively drawn to the cliffs and salt marsh.

Locally known as 'the Slunks', the whole basin flooded at high spring tides creating a rich habitat for wildlife and plants. Sea pinks and the lilac-coloured sea aster flourished and shelduck nested in disused rabbit burrows.

On the fore dunes, oystercatcher, ringed plover and little tern were common, establishing territories on the shingles surrounding the North Esk estuary.

At Gun Moo the basalt cliffs were literally alive with nesting herring gulls and fulmars during July and August, and in the gorse the distinctive song of the yellowhammer—'deil-deil-deil-tak ye'—could be heard. Occasionally a peregrine would swoop in over the cliff tops and send seabirds into panic.

Sadly, much has changed in twenty years—the seabirds have gone and the salt-marsh no longer floods, but it will always be a magical place to me—my own sort of Treasure Island.

Colin Prior

Drumochter, Perthshire

The favourite place of Alastair Mackenzie

The A9 snakes up and over the pass at Drumochter, the railway line beside it. Looking west, one sees swollen burns rushing down the hills and well-trodden paths forging deep into the wilderness.

This is a resoundingly dramatic place. I was brought up ten miles south of Drumochter, and then returned for four years to film *Monarch of the Glen* twenty miles to the north. These hills are as familiar to me as my knees. Yet every journey I take over the pass fills me with wondrous longing. I glance west and the very shape of the glen bids me to stop the car and walk: walk towards the light.

The Siren call of this wild land is always irresistible; it just sucks me in. I know Rannoch Moor is just beyond the horizon. Something powerful sings to me and it seems as if my soul is beckoned out of my chest and into the hills. Heaven is out there somewhere, I've just got to try and reach it.

If I travel up on the sleeper, I will set my alarm so as to be able to open the blind and catch Drumochter at dawn.

I have always felt that that there is something soft about this place, despite its rocky rawness. This photograph captures that. The heather seems to blanket the hard hills. I want to lie there basking in the evening sun, knowing that the rain is soon to come down from the hill beyond.

My heart is in this place. And it changes every time I see it, a shift in the light taking it from beautiful to foreboding in an instant. That is Scotland. And I love it.

Alastair Mackenzie

Tràigh Bàn, Isle of Iona

The favourite place of Sarah Heaney

The first time I visited Iona, it literally took my breath away. I thought that places like this only existed in dreams—it truly is the most beautiful, peaceful and spiritual place in the world.

Standing on Tràigh Bàn, one of many contrasting beaches on the island, I was mesmerised by the dazzling sands and the glistening waters as I breathed in the crisp sweet air. I only have to close my eyes and I'm there again…

Sarah Heaney

Greyfriars Monastery, Uddingston, Glasgow

The favourite place of Jimmy Johnstone

Over my life I have regularly visited Greyfriars Monastery and its beautiful grounds for a whole variety of reasons, but mostly for peace and quiet. I can't believe that this tranquil place is so close to the motorway. It amazes me that there is no sound of traffic at all to be heard.

On many occasions I have rung the bell in the small church behind the big house in the photograph and it would be answered by a Brother from the Franciscan Order who would invite me in for confession—though I would never see him. This has been a very important part of my life.

While walking through the grounds, I would meet a great many people who would stop and pass the time of day. I can clearly remember the statue of Our Lady in the corner of the garden overlooking the River Clyde which passes by the edge of the grounds on its way to the sea. Up until a year ago I continued to train and keep myself fit in the surrounding grounds of the Monastery.

The Brothers often said that the main house was haunted, and that they had some strange experiences within its walls with bells ringing and doors closing for no reason. All of this added to the fascination of the place for me.

Just as you come in the gate to the grounds, there is an old scout hall that is no longer in use. They used to hold discotheques there on a Sunday night. This is where I met my wife, Agnes. Even after all these years, we live only a mile or so away in Uddingston.

Andy's picture is perfect. The Monastery looks wonderful in full summer foliage but in autumn the colours are stunning. It's exactly the way in which I'd like my special place to be featured.

Loch Etive from Taynuilt, Argyllshire

The favourite place of Karen Matheson

Growing up in the little village of Taynuilt on the shores of Loch Etive was a magical experience. This picture stirs wonderful childhood memories of long summer days searching for crabs, chasing swans and eating cheese and tomato sannies (filled with sand) under the imposing beauty of Buachaille Etive Mòr. In later years it was beach barbecues and birthday parties on the boat, *Anne of Etive*, with trips up the loch to watch the sunset while otters ducked in and out of the rocks.

I was recently involved in filming a TV programme which required me to row out to the middle of the loch (with a little help) and watch the sun come up. The scene was breathtakingly beautiful, a crisp December morning, sunlight dancing on the water and mountains capped with snow. Time literally stood still. To steal a phrase from a friend and great songwriter James Grant, 'If I see this picture when I die I'll know I've landed in heaven.'

Karen Matheson

Arran Skyline, Ayrshire

The favourite place of Hugh McIlvanney

As somebody born and raised in Ayrshire, I have always had the outline of Arran against the western sky as part of the furniture of my spirit. My deep attachment is not to the island itself, though on visits there I've found it easy to appreciate the charms that have captivated other contributors to this series.

What is special for me is the sight of Arran from the mainland shore, its central presence in the majestic sweep of the Firth of Clyde, a place I have never ceased to regard as magical.

I think the vistas of the Firth are not only uniquely Scottish but, in their contours and the changes of light and perspectives, very much of the west of Scotland. Naturally in me they stir feelings of family, memories of youth, all the thousand and one effects that come with a sense of belonging.

But I believe a stranger, too, might be moved, especially if he or she looked out from the Ayrshire littoral around Barassie and Troon, as Andy Hall did to take this heartbreakingly beautiful photograph, and saw Arran and the dozen miles of intervening sea bathed in the last rays of the setting sun.

It is, of course, a view of many moods, and Arran is liable to do a Garbo and disappear altogether behind a wall of mist. But that just makes its re-emergence as welcome as seeing the face of an old friend you have been missing.

Work has caused me to be away from Scotland most of my life, but I have made a point of being a frequently returning native, so my Scottishness hasn't required strenuous maintenance. If it ever does, I'll look at Andy's picture.

Hugh McIlvanney

The East Coast of the Isle of Harris

The favourite place of Dame Elizabeth Blackadder

My visits to the Isle of Harris made a deep impression on me. Visually, it was quite stunning. The contrast between the east and west coast is quite marked, and to me the barren, rocky east coast was more striking. Perhaps these bleak, stark landscapes reminded me of my favourite early Italian paintings.

They lie south of Tarbert, along the 'Golden Road' (a far cry from the other Golden Road), a twisting, narrow road beside rocks and peat cuttings, and look east towards the island of Scalpay. Beyond, in the distance, lie the Shiant Islands.

At dawn, a pale yellow sky would gradually illuminate the dark shape of the islands, the light changing all the time, quite fantastic. In the distance, smoke from a passing ship, or did I only imagine that in a painting? Forever changing light and weather—perhaps an eagle hovering overhead, hardly moving.

This beautiful photograph brings it all back.

The King's Course, Gleneagles

The favourite place of Alan Hansen

Andy's beautiful photograph encapsulates everything I feel about Gleneagles. For me, it is a combination of golf and heaven. I was brought up in Sauchie, only half an hour away.

Golf is my first love. There is no better place to play than Gleneagles with such beautiful scenery surrounding the course. I'm very competitive, and always want to win, but at Gleneagles losing doesn't seem so bad, and that's saying something for me.

This lovely photograph, looking back towards Glendevon, will always serve as a reminder of this wonderful place. Anyone who has never played at Gleneagles is seriously missing out!

Alan Hansen

Lossiemouth, Morayshire

The favourite place of Dr Winnie Ewing

My most courageous act was to become the SNP Candidate for Moray and Nairn, to leave my comfortable, familiar Glasgow home and my well-entrenched Glasgow society, and I have no regrets. I was a stranger and they took me in.

I bought a tiny house on the Square in Lossiemouth, effectively I moved in amongst fisherfolk, well warned they would accept me or reject me. This new town, of the broad streets and the fishing harbour and market place, never stopped providing me with thrills. Happily, I was accepted and was very proud of this.

Also, of course, I had the joy of the scenery of Lossie—the two beaches, and all around lovely towns and villages of infinite variety. The world of the farmer also became my world of concern.

The people of Moray have a great sense of wit and fun and of egalitarianism. There is no more point in having airs and graces in Moray than in Glasgow.

As I joined Moray Golf Club, Findhorn Yacht Club, Nairn Sailing Club, Elgin Operatic Society, the welcome was warm.

Early mornings I often used to rise and have a stroll to the harbour. Saturday mornings usually meant an anonymous 'fry' of fish on my hall tray.

Delights galore were contained in the memories of the fishermen who had followed the fleets round the Northern Isles and to Wick, and the memories of women who served as maids in 10 Downing Street for Ramsay MacDonald. My academic husband on retirement came to live in Lossie and after his death I will never leave Moray.

Castle Campbell, Dollar Glen, Clackmannanshire

The favourite place of Barbara Dickson

This picture is beautiful and captures the lonely grandeur of Dollar Glen. I have loved Castle Campbell since I was a child in Dunfermline; we used occasionally to go to the Hillfoots as a treat, although my father had no car.

My dearest friend, Yvonne Kirkus, was the custodian of the place for many years and tramped those hills for most of her time there. Dollar Glen is truly beautiful, without being inaccessible. You don't have to drive for hours from anywhere central to enjoy its charms.

My children now look on Castle Campbell as a very special place too. Born in London and raised in England, they were reminded of half of their own heritage when we visited Yvonne.

Sadly she retired last year. I'll just have to buy a castle now!

Camusdarach, Morar, Lochaber

The favourite place of Malky McCormick

Many years ago, I set up my tent overlooking a small bay on the north-west coast of Scotland. Ever since then, my family and I regularly visit its beauty, always under canvas.

Now, when I reveal my favourite location, please don't all rush there at once! Camusdarach is a beach south of Morar, north of Arisaig. Meaning in Gaelic 'Bay of the Oaks', it is hidden from the Mallaig road by those very trees.

With the islands of Rum, Eigg, and Skye behind, look towards the bay's white sands as they climb to the spectacular sand dunes, topped with yellow broom. Eastwards, the snow-capped mountains of Lochaber are dominated by Sgurr na Ciche, a perfect conical peak.

To walk barefoot on the shore of Camusdarach is heaven on earth… with its own unique aroma.

I swam there, one summer's evening, with two seals. Even sitting in my Ayrshire studio, penning this picture of Camusdarach, I long to be there. I simply love it.

Dunkeld, Perthshire

The favourite place of Jimmy Logan

This lovely photograph is of the ancient bridge at Dunkeld. If you stand on the banks of the river that stretches down from the Cathedral and watch the fast flowing river, you will see a beauty that is timeless.

If you cross this ancient bridge and walk down the bank at the other side by the Old Toll House, you come to Birnam Woods, mentioned by William Shakespeare. Apart from the beauty of the trees, the sound of the water as it dances round the stones on the shore is a melody that has never been captured by man.

For the South African War, the Duke of Atholl raised a regiment and called it the Scottish Horse. Dunkeld is its Regimental Headquarters and I can hear the horses crossing this bridge in 1914 on their way to the war that was to end all wars.

My father spent his life in theatre, but as a young man he was called up and, because he loved horses and the smart uniform, he joined the Scottish Horse. In January 1918, he was wounded and had to have his right leg amputated. Fifty years later, when we visited Dunkeld, he pointed out the river where he was confined to barracks for three days for swimming in the fast tide against orders. He even remembered the house in the village where he was billeted as a young soldier paying 1s. 6d. a week. As I walk in Dunkeld to this day, my father is by my side as he was before a bit of shrapnel changed his life.

This photograph captures much of the special beauty and peace to be found there and as the spring changes to autumn and the colour of the trees from summer to autumn gold, I hope it makes you want to go and see its beauty for yourself.

Edinburgh from the Braid Hills

The favourite place of Ronnie Corbett

Between the ages of perhaps seven and twelve, every Sunday after lunch and morning kirk, my dad would take us—Allan, my brother, and sister Maggie—on a walk that would take in this view. He knew the route well because he was a member of the Harrison, attached to the Braids, and as a night baker probably played the course at quiet times off a handicap of three or four, so he was pretty good, certainly better than me.

No golfers on the course on a Sunday in those days but it is nice to see them in the picture now.

We would give Mum a break to put her feet up and we would walk up the Fairmilehead side, right across the Braid Hills and down the Liberton side to and from Marchmont Road. It is quite a distance when I drive it now. When we returned home fresh-faced and rosy-cheeked, we would have a delicious tea, Welsh Rarebit as only Mum could make it. She had a clever way of doing it and it turned out like a very cheesy, beautifully scrambled egg. We would then enjoy toast with homemade raspberry jam, quite delicious. Then Dad was off to the evening service at the church—on his own, I'm afraid.

Ronnie Corbett

Clachan Sands, North Uist

The favourite place of Calum Macdonald

We all have our special places of sanctuary and contemplation, where the natural world becomes a temple and where the physical and spiritual landscapes unite.

I have been coming to Clachan Sands all my life, and I have seen this place in all its changing moods and myriad contrasts. From the expansive arc of the bay, round the rocky point to Hornish, looking across to the island of Lingay and the rolling hills of Harris. From the two cemeteries denoting two eras, to the green, gentle swathes, flecked with wind-blown sand and wild flowers.

This place is special and personal, because it has always carried the lives of my ancestors. From the final resting place of generations, to the present lives that live and love and work the machair lands.

When you are here, you are beyond the restrictions of time, you hold the past as much as you wonder at each passing second, catching fleeting glimpses of the light that moves us on to something infinitely greater.

> *The light is on me, all time is here*
> *I'm going down to Clachan to stem the rush of years.*

The Wallace Monument, Stirling

The favourite place of Kenny Logan

My family farm sits underneath the Wallace Monument. I had lived there all my life until I moved to London in 1997. Every day I woke up and it marked the horizon in rain, sun or snow.

I loved the fact that when I left Stirling I could describe where I lived by the Wallace Monument. If people had been to Stirling they knew where I lived by the monument location.

In 2000 I proposed to my now wife at the top of the monument. She jokes that if she had said no, she might have had to jump off rather than walk down the steps.

The monument is a man-made structure but it is the scenery and hills around that make it so special. After the film Braveheart they built a statue of William Wallace at the entrance to the Monument. It's uncanny how much he looks like Mel Gibson!

Edzell, Angus

The favourite place of Bob Crampsey

Scottish villages as a rule tend to be workmanlike rather than beautiful, but now and again one comes along which manages to combine both qualities.

Such a one is Edzell, which impinges on the visitor at about a mile's distance from the Brechin side. Through a forest, round a bend and suddenly there is the triumphal arch guarding the entrance to Dalhousie's village.

The overwhelming impression is of spaciousness; the 'Glennie' (the Glenesk Hotel), sits back from the road as does the Inglis Memorial Hall on the other side, scene of many a keenly-fought badminton match against such as the Coventry Tool Works from that same Brechin. I hear the ghostly shuttles flying through the air but also the local Operatic Society who seemed always to prefer *The Arcadians* or *The Maid of the Mountains* to the latest Broadway success.

The golf course is one of Scotland's sleeping giants, beautiful beyond words with many glorious views of the Angus glens to compensate for the foozled shot. The breadth of the streets makes Edzell a relaxing place and if the wind is off the hills, it makes one realise that for much of the year one does not breathe air within the meaning of the act.

Down the lane that runs alongside the Post Office is the Shakkin' Brig, which moves just enough to lead to the odd uneasy thought. I have abundant memories of the place. The year of 1955 crowds in, when it did not rain in those parts from Whit Monday until almost early September. The salmon could be lifted from the North Esk, had they been worth the lifting.

I like to think I played a small part in the destiny of the village. I was up at the 'drome when we handed over to the Americans.

I played football all over the Mearns. It remains my favourite part of Scotland and I thought the very least was to take my wife there on our honeymoon. Short of 'buying the company' there was nothing more I could do. I still go back; I still find it an enchanted place.

Bob Crampsey

Ettrick Valley, Selkirk, the Borders

The favourite place of Sir David Steel

The Ettrick Valley is over twenty miles long from its top at Potburn Farm to the point where the Ettrick Water joins the Tweed outside the Royal and Ancient Burgh of Selkirk. My home has been in this beautiful valley, with its upland rugged hills of trees and heather to its low-lying pastures, since 1966.

The valley was the home of James Hogg, the Ettrick Shepherd, whose words and poetry are currently enjoying a renaissance. His grave is in Ettrick Churchyard, only hundreds of yards from where he was born.

My current home is only four miles up the valley from Selkirk, in the now restored Aikwood Tower (later anglicised by Sir Walter Scott and others to 'Oakwood'), built in the late sixteenth century. In the byre attached to the tower we currently house the James Hogg Museum.

The stretch of the Ettrick in this photograph is the town's water where, in common with other members of the Selkirk and District Angling Association, I cast an occasional optimistic fly over an ungrateful salmon.

David Steel

The Falls of Bruar, Blair Atholl, Perthshire

The favourite place of Ronnie Browne

For more than forty years, I travelled the roads of Scotland to perform the songs of Scotland in hotel lounges, farm barns, village halls and city concert halls. I couldn't possibly count the number of times I passed the sign on the A9 which pointed to the Falls of Bruar. Of course I was always in too much of a hurry driving between venues to stop. I don't even remember taking the time to read that this had been a famous beauty spot since Victorian times.

I found out just what I had been missing when, in 1981, on a short family holiday near Killiecrankie, I took the opportunity to visit the Falls for the first time to discover for myself just why so many people had been coming to the area for so long.

To say that they are breathtaking is an understatement. I don't mean it in the sense of Niagara or Victoria but just in the number of sights and sounds of water-carved grottoes and tunnels and pools encountered at every turn of the winding path up the gorge.

I particularly like the way Andy has caught the creamy, moving effect of the falling water to contrast with the rock-solid static bridge. The picture is, for me, the perfect reminder of the place and I hope that if, like me, you have passed by and not stopped, you will remedy that by not delaying any longer.

Stop, and take a hike.

Ronnie Browne

The Whinney Hill, Arthur's Seat, Edinburgh

The favourite place of Richard Demarco

The topography of Edinburgh is defined by its seven hills. The largest and most impressive is known as Arthur's Seat. It rises, in the shape of a gigantic lioness, to a height of almost one thousand feet. From its summit, a 360-degree view of Scotland's Lowlands and Highlands can be enjoyed.

However, my favourite vantage point on Arthur's Seat is not from the summit, but from the Whinney Hill at a height of 600 feet where the modern urban landscape and the suburban cityscape are hidden by the undulating grassy slopes upon which you find yourself walking in search of a view of Salisbury Crags.

Standing here, you see directly before you Edinburgh Castle as the focal point in a primeval tree-less landscape, formed by the great upsurge of a volcanic explosion which gave Edinburgh all its hills. You are looking at the steep northern slopes of a valley rising above the Hunter's Bog, and on it are the unmistakable tracks of countless generations of men and animals. These are like large drawings on the earth's surface. They lead your eye to the only man-made structure in sight. It is a veritable citadel made manifest by Edinburgh Castle's medieval walls. They are protecting the residence of kings and queens of Scotland which came into being many centuries before Holyrood Palace.

It is on these slopes of Arthur's Seat that I have begun many journeys in the spirit of exploration and pilgrimage, leading the students of the Demarco Gallery's 'Edinburgh Arts' Summer School, together with teachers from Edinburgh University's School of Scottish Studies, and artists such as Joseph Beuys, Günther Uecker, Marina Abramovi, Ivan Illich, Paul Neagu and Per Kirkeby. I planned these journeys to help alter the course of Scottish art by incorporating the prehistoric monuments of Callanish and the Ring of Brodgar, statements which aspire to the condition of sculpture, whilst acting over many millennia as megalithic lunar and solar observatories.

Beyond Corstorphine Hill lies the quintessential 'Road to the Isles'. It is a drovers' road and it was travelled by Roman legionaries and their Pictish adversaries as well as Celtic saints and scholars. I recognise it as 'the Road to Meikle Seggie'. Now designated as a farm, Meikle Seggie was at one time one of Scotland's villages—a lost settlement which we cannot afford to forget if we take seriously the Scotland celebrated in bardic poetry, folksong and travellers' tales.

Andy Hall's photograph brings into sharp focus that dramatic moment when the first image of Edinburgh Castle appeared unexpectedly, growing organically out of a timeless primeval Scottish landscape. Looking closely at the photograph, you can see the world of Macbeth, Mary Queen of Scots and the Celtic and Roman inhabitants of Arthur's Seat.

This photograph could be part of your dream as Camelot come true. Under the bright light of summer morning sunshine, there is revealed the reality of a landscape in which history and mythology are inextricably intertwined.

Richard Demarco

Ibrox Stadium, Glasgow

The favourite place of Alastair Johnston

Growing up in Glasgow, I always recall my Dad referring to the red-brick facade of Ibrox Stadium as 'the bricks and mortar that guard a cherished past'.

This was indeed the portal that towered over the playing field where on many memorable Saturday afternoons the relative success of the charges of the 'men in the famous light blue' would determine your mood for several days; whether or not it was even worthwhile going out with your girlfriend that night, and, most assuredly, whether or not you would be the purveyor or the victim of the bragging and harassment that would inevitably be encountered at school, college, or work on the following Monday morning.

There was something solid and reassuring about the edifice at Ibrox. For many Scots, it was a symbol that bore a direct connection to your father and grandfather before you and probably to your own son and grandson as they, in turn, would be forced to listen to the tales of heroics from 'bygone days of yore'. (No matter how 'blue-tinted' these recollections proved to be.)

This particular photograph displays Ibrox under the typical grey, foreboding skies that were so predictable and prevalent in Glasgow that they, along with ambition and adventure, motivated me to emigrate to sunnier climes. However, as my mind drifts back to Govan, as it inevitably does on match days, no matter where I am in the world, I can only see in my own mind blue skies over the stadium on every occasion when Rangers triumph.

Kilbride Bay, near Tighnabruaich, Cowal

The favourite place of Jackie Bird

I first stumbled across Kilbride Bay twenty years ago when visiting nearby Tighnabruaich. The locals call it Ostel Bay, and it's one of their best-kept secrets. The horseshoe-shaped bay can only be reached by a walk of about a mile cross-country, the last part of which is a bounce across peat bogs, dodging ankle-breaking rabbit holes as you go. However the beauty and serenity that await you are well worth the trek.

The bay is about 400 metres wide. It nestles between the Argyll hills on one side, a rocky outlet on the other, with the majesty of Arran in front.

The sea-bed is flat for a good distance, which means that on a sunny day the incoming tide warms up nicely, allowing you to attempt that rare pastime—a swim in Scottish waters.

However the bay is also as breathtaking on a chilly November morning, or a dreich rainy afternoon in March, as it is in the height of summer. It must be the sense of being cosseted by the land—it's a comforting place.

It's also a place of many happy memories—of romantic walks, family picnics, of my dad giving his pink-faced, tired-out grandchildren piggy-backs across the dunes back to the car.

Andy's photograph has captured the seclusion and tranquillity of the landscape. The colours are incredible. The framing of the walk to the beach using the long grass is so welcoming—an invitation to a spectacular wide-screen production.

I know there are grander beaches in Scotland where the sands are whiter, the water more blue, but for me Kilbride is not only a place of beauty, it's got soul.

Loch Tummel, Perthshire

The favourite place of Sir Ian Wood

Bohally House on Loch Tummel in Perthshire is our new weekend home—an ideal country retreat which will be well used by our extended families.

The view up the loch from Bohally is almost a mirror image of the famous 'Queen's View'— a magnificent vista with the shimmering soft light on the vast loch surrounded by the majestic beauty of Scottish mountains, forests and open moors. It is truly a 'rest and be thankful' home, soothed by the constantly lapping water, the shrill cries of the bird life (ospreys nesting just across the loch), the swans, the geese, the ducks, and the vast array of wildlife.

Andy has captured all of this magnificently in this sunrise shot looking up the loch—the beauty, peace and tranquillity of a breaking dawn on Loch Tummel.

Daylight brings a kaleidoscope of changing colours—all shades of green, yellow, brown and blue—depending on the time of day and the changing weather. On a sunny day, with the rays dancing over the loch, this is one of Scotland's great beauty spots.

Greenock

The favourite place of Alan Sharp

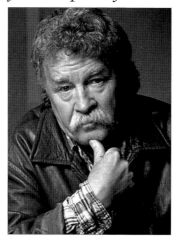

Greenock's location, where the Clyde widens to estuary, has always been its crowning glory, what elevated it from a modest provincial town to one of the holy places, worthy of bardic celebration.

As a boy, this view, minus half a dozen high rises, would appear as we trampled home from the hills, foot-sodden, sock-ruined, with the aroma of the gorse macaroon-sweet in the air.

We did not linger long to savour its splendours: the hope of Welsh rarebit for tea and the urgings of gravity sent us hurtling homewards, unheeding.

But the imprinting remains metaphor as much as memory; the town clustering, the river flowing, the hills abiding; a secular psalm, the true place you will not find down on any map.

We, all of us, attach significance to our origins, or shaping source, sometimes embittered, sometimes sentimental, often both. My own feelings are best expressed in the town song whose doggerel can still be sung with genuine emotion these many years later:

> *It's been a while since I was there*
> *In dear old Greenock Toon,*
> *But I'll be going back again*
> *An' I'll be going soon.*
> *I'll look oot across the Clyde*
> *High flowin' tae the sea,*
> *An' I'll hear the birdies singin'*
> *In the Green Oak Tree.*

Alan Sharp

Aberdeen Coastline

The favourite place of Willie Miller

Since I was 16, I have enjoyed the Aberdeen coastline. It is a part of Aberdeen that I have used both professionally and recreationally. It is an area of outstanding beauty, irrespective of the prevailing weather conditions.

With Pittodrie only a stone's throw away from the coastline, it is a place Aberdeen Football Club takes advantage of for the training and rehabilitation of injured players. It has been used in bad weather in the depths of winter when no other facilities were available to us—as long as the tide was out, of course!

And in rehabilitation, I have had my fair share of jogging in the icy water to aid the healing process, and on every occasion I have been struck by the natural aspect of the coastline, whether the sun was shining or wild waves were thundering towards the shore. I also have business interests overlooking the harbour, so on a daily basis I am again confronted with the outstanding views that lie before me.

With the wonderful scenery in both good and bad weather, this is an area that keeps drawing me back.

Lunan Bay, Angus

The favourite place of Isla Dewar

There is a stillness about Lunan Bay. We used to walk along that shore a lot, having long rambling mobile conversations. We rarely saw a soul. There is always something magical about having a beach to yourselves.

Years ago, we brought in New Year there. This photograph brings that night back to me, not just how it looked, but how it smelled, sounded. It was cold, and wonderfully clear. Not surprisingly, there was nobody else about. The moon spread long, shimmering paths on the sea. The sand looked bleached. Looking at the picture, I am back there with the smell of salt air, sounds of water and the odd gull floating, white in the darkness.

But more than all that, I can recapture vividly the very keen specialness of a moment. Two of us, on a beach, waiting for a new year to start, knowing that soon our lives would change. We toasted the bells with coffee from a flask, and shortbread. Four days later my son was born. In years to come we'd take him, and later his brother, to join our mobile conversations there.

Isla Dewar

New Deer Parish Church, Aberdeenshire

The favourite place of Steve Forbes

This photograph evokes the moral compass that guided my grandfather, B C Forbes, who was born and raised in New Deer. He recognised what today too many don't: there is a moral foundation to business; to succeed, you must meet the needs and wants of others. To fulfill your ambitions and aspirations in a democratic free-enterprise society, you also serve others. In serving only yourself, he believed, you corrode your own soul.

In the first issue of Forbes, which he founded in 1917, thirteen years after he immigrated to America, B C Forbes wrote, 'Business was originated to produce happiness, not to pile up millions.'

The Clyde above Hyndford Bridge, near Lanark

The favourite place of James Cosmo

I visited the Clyde at Hyndeford Bridge many times between the ages of 18 and 23: in the summer to fish the runs for the brownies, and in the winter to hunt the lady of the stream, the greyling. The peace to be found there was in such contrast to my home in Clydebank and John Brown's and Arnott Young's where I once worked. But that river, teeming with wildlife, was a refreshment for the soul.

I have fished in many parts of the world—New Zealand for giant rainbows, Mexico for marlin—but if I had just one day to spend on the river it would be as it was in my youth—a fly rod on the Clyde.

Many times I have thought to return, but to return to a place that once brought happiness and contentment is a dangerous thing to do. So that place will remain unsullied and pure in my dreams.

James Cosmo

Callanish Stones, Isle of Lewis

The favourite place of Kenneth McKellar

This great stone circle on the Isle of Lewis was known to Herodotus as 'The Great Winged Temple of the Northern Isles'.

Erected almost 5000 years ago by pre-Celtic people of Iberian stock and dedicated to sun-worship, they are aligned north and south towards the Pole Star. They have watched the Stone Age merge into the Age of Bronze and they mark the dead of both.

Many years ago when I stood within the Callanish Circle for the first time, I felt a trembling, a thrill throughout my being, and this reappears with each visit. Standing there on the geology of twenty million years, one is forcibly faced once again with one's insignificance.

Callanish has had a great influence on my life—a house named 'Callanish' in Argyll, a house named 'Callanish' by my daughter in Australia, and lately a granddaughter named 'Callan'.

What more can I say?

The Gogo Burn, Largs, Ayrshire

The favourite place of Daniela Nardini

The Gogo Burn runs through the grounds of my family home in Largs. To me it is the most special and peaceful place in the world. It's home!

Whenever I return, I wander through the woods to the old footbridge, stand in the centre, look eastwards in the mornings and westwards in the evenings, each creating a totally different effect, but sharing the calming and relaxing sound of the burn just under my feet.

Daniela Nardini

The Garden of Buchan, Old Deer, Aberdeenshire

The favourite place of Jack Webster

For the finale of the BBC drama-documentary about my childhood, *As Time Goes By*, I wandered alone among the ruins of the historic Abbey of Deer, three miles from the Aberdeenshire village of Maud, where I grew up.

As the final sweep of music I chose Elgar's deeply moving *Nimrod* and could feel history washing over me. For this haven of peace had stood since 1219, replacing an earlier monastery founded in the sixth century by St Columba and St Drostan, who brought Christianity to these parts.

It is an oasis amid the naked beauty of Buchan, the silence broken by the babble of the River Ugie as it wends towards the sea at Peterhead. These monasteries were the local inns of the day, offering the traveller a safe place from the highway robber.

In my childhood of the 1930s, the Roman Catholic priesthood came on a regular pilgrimage to this place, disgorged from the Buchan train which stopped at the little wooden platform just once a year. To the child it was a fearsome excitement. For the purpose of my 1987 television film, they re-enacted the procession, strange and haunting.

In glinting stone and sombre tree, Andy Hall's picture captures the mood within this spiritual home of Buchan, where I still come from time to time in search of peace and harmony.

Jack Webster

Haley Brae, Largs, Ayrshire

The favourite place of Billy McNeill

My first memory of the view over the Cumbraes from Haley Brae was as a young player with Celtic, travelling to Seamill Hydro for the first time. The spectacular vista of the island of Great Cumbrae and the Firth of Clyde caught my attention and has stayed with me ever since.

Often I stop the car when I reach the Brae and spend a few moments peacefully taking in what I consider to be one of the most wonderful sights I have encountered in my travels over the world.

The combination of the far Argyll shores, the multicoloured sea and the Cumbrae islands combine to make a picture that is typical of Scotland. I take great pride in being Scottish and I feel that this view from Haley Brae truly represents the beauty of our land and is a must for visitors from all over the globe.

Plockton, Wester Ross

The favourite place of Jonathan Watson

My wife used to visit Plockton as a child and loved the place. We travelled there a few weeks before our son, Jack, was born and, since then, we have made it a regular family destination during the summer months. It's a great place to relax.

Stonehouse Farm, Airth, Stirlingshire

The favourite place of Dr Tom Sutherland

Though I did not recognise it at the time, growing up on Stonehouse Farm, right on the banks of the River Forth, was idyllic.

To the east, across the River Forth, lay the Ochil Hills, and during the holidays from Grangemouth High School it was my summer duty to be up around 4.30 am and well on my way by five to the banks of the river to round up the cows for the morning milking.

I clearly recall stopping by the gate of the pasture, putting one foot on the lowest bar and singing in full stentorian voice 'Oh What a Beautiful Morning', one of my very favourite songs from the musical Oklahoma. And looking across the Forth, as does this photo, there lay the Ochils.

It was not till I had been some years in the US and had seen at first hand both Oklahoma and the even more scenic Colorado where I now live, that I returned to the native heath and, more mature now, appreciated the true beauty of the Scottish scene.

Driving across the Kincardine Bridge, I took a trip along the foothills of the Ochils by Alloa and Dollar, thence to Stirling. The hills are even more spectacular up close, but my favourite view was still from that five-barred gate, looking into the rising sun, and appreciating the coming challenge of a new day.

In this photograph, the bales of straw illustrate the marvellous fertility of the soil on Stonehouse Farm. The pasture from which I brought in the cows in the early morning is now sown to grain, the dairy herd is no more, and I see the Ochils on my visits home today as in this scene. But the memories flow into each other of that glorious view, and will live in my head till my dying day.

Tom Sutherland

House for an Art Lover, Bellahouston Park, Glasgow

The favourite place of Carol Smillie

Living very close to Bellahouston Park, I watched with interest as this Charles Rennie Mackintosh-designed house was built a few years ago.

Everything about it appeals to me, the windows, the setting, the walled garden and the delicious food in the café, but my favourite part is the Music Room with its full-length screen-prints and embroideries on the French windows, the piano and the sheer light, bright, airy feeling.

I'm there most weeks of the year for photo shoots, interviews, concerts or just having lunch.

It says everything about Glasgow's style and it is my special place.

Hoy and Gutter Sound, Orkney

The favourite place of Sir Ludovic Kennedy

Although I have the happiest memories of my childhood in Edinburgh and summer holidays on the seafront at Nairn and in Islay, the photograph I have chosen is that of the east side of the Island of Hoy which lies on the west side of Scapa Flow in the Orkney Islands.

In the centre of the frame lies the habitation of Lyness which fronts on to Gutter Sound, two places that still have a very special place in my heart. During the last war, Gutter Sound was the anchorage of the destroyer flotillas of the Home Fleet, among them HMS Tartar in which I served from 1940-42. It was the harbour from which we set out to take part in the Norwegian campaign, to escort the Arctic convoys to Russia, to chase the Bismarck and to hunt for the Tirpitz: and the place where, on return from perhaps two weeks at sea, mail from family and friends awaited us. It was our only link with home, and I recall we couldn't open the letters fast enough.

Not that there was much to do after we had anchored. Admiral Beatty, who was at Scapa in the first war, called it the most damnable place on earth and most of the navy agreed. Hoy was almost treeless, just heather and grass, seabirds and sheep, and across Gutter Sound the wind fiercely blew, often for days on end. At Lyness there were no women, shops, restaurants, just a couple of canteens that dispensed warm beer, a hall for film shows and the occasional concert party, and a brace of football fields that too often fathered the signal, All Grounds Unfit For Play.

But on board the ship, we fed well, and drink and tobacco were duty free (cigarettes a shilling for twenty, gin two pence a glass). Sometimes in the evenings, we would entertain or be entertained in the flotilla's wardrooms and dress up as Tartars, Eskimos, Bedouins; or there were evenings of film shows, which were often improved by the last reel appearing first and upside down. And we sang songs too:

> *Oh, we had to carry Carrie to the ferry,*
> *And the ferry carried Carrie to the shore,*
> *And the reason that we had to carry Carrie was*
> *Poor Carrie couldn't carry any more.*

There were other compensations, especially in summer when the hills of Hoy were touched with purples and greens and the Flow sparkled blue in the morning sun; at night too when the Northern Lights wove pale patterns in the sky the place had a rare beauty. There were afternoons when some of us would walk the two miles to Longhope to buy fresh eggs or lobsters. Or I might take my fishing rod ashore, climb a hill above the anchorage, on the other side of which lay an attractive trout loch, and there spend a couple of contented hours away from all navy sights and sounds, though every half hour or so, I had to mount the hill to make sure that the *Tartar* was not flying the Blue Peter, the signal for recall.

I have been back to Scapa several times since, once to make a documentary film on the place which included an interview with the engineer officer of the U-boat which in 1939 had penetrated the Flow and sunk the battleship *Royal Oak* with huge loss of life. On every occasion, though, I find it's the happy things I remember about my life there sixty years ago, especially the camaraderie of fellow officers, and despite the wartime drawbacks, I still find the place retains a magic all its own.

Ludovic Kennedy

King's College Quadrangle, Old Aberdeen
The favourite place of Buff Hardie

I spent four years in the 1950s as a student at King's College, Old Aberdeen, which was a wonderful setting for one's salad days. From almost every angle it is marvellously photogenic and in selecting a photograph it is perhaps a little perverse of me to ask for nothing more spectacular than the old well which is a feature of the College quadrangle.

Its most avid admirer could never claim that the well contributed a lot to the education of the mid twentieth-century undergraduate. You could lean against it; you could perch on it and chat; and you could look down into it. It was, and is, a solid stone structure, sunk to a considerable depth, and it has an attraction, as low-lying water tends to have, for low-denomination coins of the realm, tossed down from above. Over a period these coins—and their value—could mount up, and I can recall one desperate student who, having worked his way through his entire grant in the Union bar long before the end of term, got himself lowered down the well and collected a sizeable sum in small coins with which to finance his next pint.

Many years later I took part in a BBC Television programme called *The Antiques Inspectors*. Presented by Carol Vorderman, it was a variation on *The Antiques Roadshow* and it involved a team of antiques experts visiting a town or city and assessing antiques that were brought before them in private houses and other locations. One of the cities they visited was Aberdeen, where my role was that of native Aberdonian who acted as a guide to the team as they made their way about the city.

At one point they visited King's College and its fifteenth-century chapel. I had to show Carol Vorderman round the policies, and in doing so I took her to the well. We looked down into it, and the cameraman succeeded in getting a shot which revealed that the practice of tossing coins into the well still continues. That being so, I told the story of the impecunious student who had descended into the well in pursuit of his beer money. As I ended the story, I said on impulse, 'That chap is now a Judge in the Court of Session.' It wasn't true, but I plead poetic licence. It was surely a permissible fiction, and it seemed like a nice way to end the story. The programme director thought so too, and the fictitious ending survived the editing of the tape. In other words, he kept it in.

The programme was transmitted a few weeks later, and the following day I received a card through the post. All it said was, 'I did not remove the money from the King's College well.' It was signed by the only Court of Session judge who is a graduate of Aberdeen University.

Buff Hardie

Ettrick Bay, Isle of Bute

The favourite place of Tam Cowan

The more I look at this picture the more I think Andy Hall must have indulged in a little bit of trick photography. Clouds at Ettrick Bay? No way. The Ettrick Bay I so fondly remember boasted non-stop blue skies, crystal-clear water and the most incredible sandy shore that meant you could walk halfway to Ireland without getting your knees wet.

I first enjoyed this view as a three-year-old when my dad went on a 25th-anniversary camping trip to Rothesay with the 17th Motherwell BB Company and I tagged along. Well, it was either that or go to Disney World with my mum and wee sister... Aye, right!

Ever since that unforgettable moment (the Glasgow Fair of 1972), the Isle of Bute—and particularly Ettrick Bay—has had a special place in my heart, and this photo triggers so many special memories. The taste of the Currie's Red Kola they sold from one of the tents. The joy of finding a freshwater spring on the beach. And, of course, the tearoom at the far end of the bay (still there to this day) that sold the most fabulous cream cakes.

I still return to Ettrick Bay at least once a year and the sights, the sounds and the smells are always exactly the same. Only one thing has changed over the years... where did that little boat suddenly appear from?

Guess I'll just have to keep going back until I find out...

Braid Hills, Edinburgh

The favourite place of John Greig

My abiding memory of Braid Hills Golf Course is of regular Sunday morning walks with my son Murray as a little boy, a friend of mine and his dog. Even though these walks were thirty years ago, I can still see Murray, full of energy, running ahead of us all.

I have also played golf at Braid Hills several times and on each occasion I have been captivated by the view over Edinburgh. With the Fife coast beyond the Firth of Forth, the unmistakable shape of Edinburgh Castle, and, to the right of where Andy took the picture, Arthur's Seat, then on towards Cockenzie and the East Lothian coastline, I still hold a place in my heart for this view.

As a player with Rangers, I was expected to keep fit in my own time as well as training with the club, particularly in the close season. I took part in many solitary training runs over the Braid Hills countryside at that time.

I have lived in Glasgow for twenty-six years but I still retain a real affection for the beautiful city of Edinburgh, the place of my birth, and the wonderful views from the Braid Hills.

Invergowrie Bay, Dundee

The favourite place of Michael Marra

This view of Newburgh from the other side of the majestic River Tay takes me back to my childhood when my mother took my brothers, my sister and myself to Invergowrie Bay. I was reading Tom Sawyer at the time, which had a great effect on me, and in the early evening the Newburgh lights transformed the village into a Mississippi River Boat. This was probably reinforced by the fact that one of the 'Fifies' featured big paddles, seriously moustachioed men and girls in their finery of the '50s.

This view is from Kingoodie, next to the flooded quarry. They said it was bottomless, and that there was a house at the bottom. It's a very dreamy place with beautiful smells and I returned many times. It was a great place to go with a girl, as I was able to point out the Pyramids and over past Wormit, the edge of China. It gave me the chance to seem both knowledgeable and sensitive.

The photographer obviously has a feeling for the Blues.

Lady Mary's Walk, Crieff, Perthshire

The favourite place of Denis Lawson

This is pretty well a perfect shot of Lady Mary's Walk for me; taken at just the right time of year, the autumn. The colours and the light are just as I carry them in my head when I'm away.

This spot has strong personal associations for my family and myself. Since the age of three, I've loved this walk along the banks of the River Earn which I swam in throughout my childhood (only in the summers of course!). Indeed as recently as last year I had an invigorating dip.

For the first few years that I lived in London I was compelled to return to see this view as it changed through each season. It's a constantly changing canvas, no matter how often you visit it.

Port Appin, Argyllshire

The favourite place of Kirsty Young

The view from the mainland at Port Appin across Loch Linnhe and onto Lismore brings back golden memories of a weekend I spent there in September of 1998. The simplicity and strength of the landscape, broken only by a helpful wee lighthouse, is perfect.

When I'm home in Scotland, I treasure the humour and the fresh air and on that weekend I had plenty of both.

Kirsty Young.

Cruden Bay Golf Course, Aberdeenshire

The favourite place of Fiona Kennedy

There are few places in the world where I look out of the window and feel 'I'm home'. The view from our chalet at Cruden Bay makes me feel exactly like that, despite the fact that I'm a west coast girl!

I look down on what appears to be a green lunar landscape, all dewy and mysterious in the early morning, the light often most stunning at 5 am. No one about, just the distant movement of the North Sea beyond the sand dunes, an occasional ship sailing by to the Orkneys or Shetland Islands. Peace!

Although you can't see it in Andy's wonderful shot, to the left are the haunting and spectacular ruins of Slains Castle which attract Bram Stoker fans from all over the world.

This natural golf links course is amongst the finest in the world and keen golfers beat a path to this place where my husband and children love to play. They just walk down to the first tee and off they go, hail, rain or shine!

Often I stand at the kitchen window preparing a meal and get carried away with this spectacular vista. I watch golfers come and go and think how lucky I am.

Fiona Kennedy

Dunure Castle, Ayrshire

The favourite place of Lorraine McIntosh

As a child growing up in the heart of Ayrshire, I will never forget the first time I saw the beach at Dunure. There are other more spectacular beaches in Scotland, but when I saw this one I claimed it as my own. I couldn't believe that this was in fact Ayrshire—no pits or factories, just rocks and shore.

If you are lucky enough to catch the place on a winter's day with the sun peeking through the clouds, as in this picture, maybe you will understand the beauty of the place.

I return to it time and time again, now with my children, and, who knows, maybe one day they will return with theirs!

Lorraine McIntosh

Langholm, Dumfriesshire

The favourite place of Gregor Fisher

Langholm—a place that made a huge impact on an adolescent boy and taught him the value of friendship and humour! A place that not only stirs the heart with its beauty but welcomes you back after years away from her, as though you had been gone for only a moment.

Lamlash Golf Course, Isle of Arran

The favourite place of Craig Brown

As a teenager in the late '50s, I spent many hours while on holiday playing golf on the attractive, hilly Lamlash Golf Course. Vivid in my memory are the sights from the vantage points on the course, particularly the first green and second tee.

Having travelled extensively throughout the world, I feel I am in a position to make value judgements on the scenery here in Scotland. When I say that one of the most delightful views is from Lamlash Golf Course across the bay and Holy Isle towards the Ayrshire Coast, I feel I am speaking with authority.

The photograph, because of the monochromatic light, and with a ship in the bay is, in my opinion, quite exquisite and a compliment to the consummate skill of Andy Hall. I am most indebted to Andy for providing me with such a poignant reminder of my youth on the tranquil island of Arran.

Portnahaven, Isle of Islay

The favourite place of Angus Roxburgh

When Andy asked me to name the part of Scotland that meant most to me, it was a toss-up between the red-earthed Mearns of my youth, where I went to school with him (I have some of his beautiful photographs of the area on the wall of my office in Brussels), and the place I have returned to at least twice a year for the past quarter-century—the Isle of Islay.

Islay won. It was my wife's family that originally came from there, and it's there that I return to in my mind when I am in far-flung places, for it is the perfect antidote to the turmoil and change that a news reporter deals with every day.

What I love about Islay is its ancient, unchanging landscape. And Andy has captured that brilliantly in this unusual view of my adopted village, Portnahaven. Look at those primeval rocks in the foreground, bulging out of the sea like hippopotamus hide, rubbed smooth by thousands of years of pounding tides and storms.

The fishermen's cottages are only a hundred or so years old, but that's also quintessential Islay—a ribbon of white against blue sky. Usually my view from 'home' is from one of these houses, looking out across the rocks to the Atlantic Ocean. Maybe it's that contrast that makes Islay special: the peaceful, ancient land, anchored in a restless ocean.

The 17th Green at Loch Lomond Golf Club

The favourite place of Dougie Donnelly

Just half an hour's drive from central Glasgow, Loch Lomond has always held a special place in the affections of my fellow Glaswegians. I fondly remember day trips with my family as a youngster with picnics on the shores of the loch, but now I am most often in this beautiful place to play one of the world's greatest golf courses.

I remember interviewing the course designer, Tom Weiskopf, when the course first opened, and complimenting him on a superb job of integrating a golf course into such a glorious setting. He immediately insisted that his job had been easy, that he had never seen such a stunning piece of land.

The view across the loch from the 17th green lifts my spirits every time I see it. I think the combination of loch, trees, the distant hills, Rossdhu House and the old castle is simply breathtaking, especially on such a beautiful day as this when the blue sky and slightly threatening cloud formation just add to the beauty of the view.

And if you can walk off with a par 3, so much the better!

Dougie Donnelly

The Kyles of Bute, Cowal

The favourite place of Michelle Mone

This photograph of the Kyles of Bute perfectly encapsulates the beauty and tranquillity of Scotland. We may complain about receiving more than our share of rainfall but this is one of the reasons that we have such spectacular scenery.

While standing at the viewpoint looking down the Kyles of Bute it is easy to forget the hustle, bustle and stress of work and city living. A landscape such as this has not been altered by time or technology. Its beauty is breathtaking and will always hold a special place in my heart.

Michelle G Mone

Millport, Great Cumbrae Island, Ayrshire

The favourite place of Bill Paterson

Is there anything more difficult than choosing one place in all of Scotland? So keep it simple and go back to childhood.

I spent every August for nearly twenty years in Millport on the Isle of Cumbrae and even in those busy weeks there was always something lonely and wild at this spot just round Portachur Point from the West Bay. The dark volcanic rocks, the reddish shingle and the wonderful view of Arran make it almost Hebridean, and it's only thirty miles by seagull from Sauchiehall Street! You could even see basking sharks here.

This photograph really captures those textures and that restless firth. I love that dusting of snow on Arran. Most Augusts we missed the snow!

Lochgelly Loch, Fife

The favourite place of Jim Leishman

For me, Lochgelly Loch holds many fond memories from childhood and growing up. As a youngster, I spent many happy times camping beside the loch. Myself and several friends learned to swim in there and we would spend hours fishing for pike and perch during the school holidays.

As I grew up, I also learned to water-ski on the loch and, after several dunkings, I eventually managed to stay standing! The loch also has strong family connections as myself, my father, brother and sister would go for long walks in the area.

To me, Lochgelly Loch is a place of peace and tranquillity, where I can escape from the world of football for a while!

Lochgoilhead, Cowal

The favourite place of Tony Roper

The first time I set eyes on this entrancing natural wickerwork of mossy banks, golden trees and sun-dappled rocks that leads to the cave of Rob Roy in Lochgoilhead, Argyll, I thought for a twinkling that I had passed through some mystical fairy portal and found myself in the enchanted forest that Shakespeare described in *A Midsummer Night's Dream*.

I fully expected Oberon, Titania and Puck to appear from the myriad of colours that assailed my eyes. I could hear their voices in the rustle of a million russet-stained autumn leaves and their laughter tinkling in the sound of the lucid liquid that rushed from a hundred tiny waterfalls. This surely is where fairies live, I concluded.

Then I remembered that I was a product of the no-nonsense Glaswegian culture that laughed at such things. On the other hand…

The image captured here sets the scene perfectly for me until I can return and surround myself with the sounds and smells of this perfect piece of Scotland.

The River Endrick, Fintry, Stirlingshire

The favourite place of Annie Ross

Many years ago, when I was living in London and not at the pinnacle of my health, my dear brother Jim came to see me. 'I'm taking you up to Scotland to get re-energised,' he said. 'It's a place called Fintry, you'll love it.' I had never heard of Fintry but I got to know it well.

Jim had rented a small estate that consisted of a house, a grass tennis court (somewhat run-down), a vegetable garden and a small burn where you could fish for trout. There were many various colours of rhododendrons, a bluebell dell and a small waterfall.

At the end of the day, I would watch as the local doctor pulled up in his car to the river bank. He would go to the boot and take out his fishing rod, walk slowly down to the Endrick and cast. He was a remarkable man, very gentle, and he had been in a Japanese prisoner of war camp. He had seen and endured many things.

With the sunset casting a pink glow in the sky, the air so clear, it gave me a feeling of complete peace.

I will always have a warm place in my heart for Fintry.

Annie Ross

Hawick, the Borders

The favourite place of Sir Chay Blyth

There are two 'happenings' in Hawick that involve almost everyone born there from a very early age. One is rugby and the other is the Common Riding. The latter dates from the time of the Battle of Flodden, fought between the English and the Scots in 1513. The Scots came second! However they were not to be completely outdone.

In 1514 the English, on their way back home, camped at Hornshole just outside Hawick. It took a long time in those days to move armies, what with the pillaging, raping and not to mention the drinking that went on. Whilst the English were camping at Hornshole, a group of Callants from around the Border Towns gathered together and charged through the English lines. They probably didn't do much harm but the English banner (flag) was captured by a Hawick Callant who rode like fury with it back to Hawick.

The Battle of Flodden and the capturing of the banner has become a re-enactment through the Hawick Common Riding ceremonies, the ancient custom of riding round the boundaries of the common land. This was to make sure no one encroached on the land and people didn't forget where the boundaries were.

The Common Riding takes place every year and up to four hundred riders ride to the boundaries at any one time. A Cornet (a young unmarried man), who is elected by his peers each year, leads the riders. The ride-outs, as they are called, take place over a six-week period during May and June; they are always on a Tuesday and Saturday. The main ride-out consists of a 24-mile ride, and at the half point the riders and horses rest for two hours. Family and friends join them for the break and consume lots of alcohol, just like they would have done in 1514!

These rides are magnificent, with great camaraderie, and the countryside is so beautiful. The routes are allowed through the generosity of the local farmers and landowners.

Felicity, my wife and I, stay at a great holiday complex called Headshaw Farm (near Ashkirk, about five miles outside Hawick) with our horses. We have holiday accommodation and stabling for the horses, but much more than that, thanks to the owners Nancy and Gordon Hunter, we can ride over their land and onto the Buccleuch Rides, again made possible by the landowner, the Duke of Buccleuch.

The scenery is stunning, and seen from the back of a horse it is, for me, one of life's great pleasures. We go on these hacks in between the ride-outs just to keep the horses fit and to enjoy what is one of the very best experiences in life.

Morinsh, Ballindalloch, Speyside

The favourite place of Eileen McCallum

Morinsh in Ballindalloch holds a very special place in my heart. For many years our family had a cottage here and we opened our front door to Ben Rinnes every morning of the holidays, summer and winter. Andy has captured its majesty covered in snow against an incredible sky.

How grateful we should be for our country's wilder places, where time seems to stand still. The landscape of the North East has changed little since my childhood.

Eileen McCallum

Sannox Glen, Isle of Arran

The favourite place of Richard Wilson

This view of Glen Sannox brings back many happy times there on family holidays. We stayed at a small hotel called Ingledene run by Peggy and Gilbert McKinnon. Every time the bus arrived Peggy would come down the drive wiping the flour from her hands—she was a wonderful cook and wonderful hotelier.

Glen Sannox was a beautiful place as the photograph so brilliantly shows. There was excellent walking in the hills behind the house and I particularly remember going out with Gilbert (a shepherd) and his dogs, a very exciting task for a young boy!

Richard Wilson

Uath Lochans, Glenfeshie, Badenoch

The favourite place of Cameron McNeish

There is a natural dynamic between forest and mountain, one that is generally sadly lacking in Scotland. Although many of the trees that surround Uath Lochans in Glenfeshie are exotic conifers, there is still a resonance of those ancient days when much of the Scottish Highlands was blanketed in forest.

The lovely lochans here often reflect the hills behind and their moods and colours reflect something of that special aura for which the Highlands are renowned.

In the lighting, Andy has certainly caught the magic of the Uath Lochans.

Cameron McNeish

The West Sands, St Andrews, Fife

The favourite place of Hazel Irvine

The West Sands at St Andrews have been a special place for me ever since I was a student at University in the 'Auld Grey Toon'.

I went for long walks there with my friends and it was also a place I loved to experience on my own.

Whenever I am back in St Andrews, be it for work or pleasure, I always make time to stroll along the beach, look out to the sea and watch the town getting smaller on the horizon with every step.

Ullapool, Wester Ross

The favourite place of Rikki Fulton

Ullapool, a name the Norsemen gave it, was founded in 1788. The very drive through to greet the scenery makes it worthwhile. Summer or winter, this little village maintains the warmth of the people who live here and will happily chat to you in English or the Gaelic.

One of our visits found us close to Loch Torridon to stretch our legs and we were visited by a brilliant rainbow which was bold enough to present itself and enter the driving seat of our car. But what matters when good luck comes!

My wife, Kate, and I have visited many times and look forward to further visits in that delightful village.

After all, you can't get higher than a rainbow!

Rikki Fulton.

Gigha and Jura, Argyllshire

The favourite place of Dougray Scott

This photograph of Gigha and Jura conjures up so many special memories for me, from an early age. I used to visit Gigha with my family over a period of many years and whenever I come here, I always feel incredibly happy and alive.

I remember the clear turquoise waters and beautiful gardens on the isle. I remember the journey to get here from Glasgow, past Loch Fyne and down the Kintyre peninsula. It is my favourite journey in the world.

When I stand here looking at this most extraordinary sunset, I feel so fortunate to be Scottish. Whenever anyone asks me where they should visit in Scotland, I always send them here. It also reminds me of journeys with my father.

Dougray Scott

Gairloch, Wester Ross

The favourite place of Gavin Esler

Gairloch is the Scotland of my childhood, the country where the air is so clean it intoxicates you, the sea so clear you can see the sea urchins beneath the oars of your boat.

It is a country where the summer evenings never end. They go from the gold tones of the setting sun kissing the sea, in this photograph, to the purple of the gloaming.

I would stand at the very spot in Andy's photograph, feeling the cold seawater and sand between my toes, staring south to the mountains. I would dream of catching salmon (I never did) but have to settle for small trout and eels which flicked themselves into knots around my line.

I always knew, even as a small boy, that I would leave Scotland and travel the world. I always knew I would, in one sense, never leave completely. I am still there in Gairloch, still trying to get a salmon out of the burn, still watching the seals near the old lighthouse to the north, still sleeping in a tent among the sand dunes, supping the air like a fine malt, enjoying the best sleep of my life.

Home. Belonging. Scotland. A place of the heart.

Biographies in Brief

Kaye Adams has worked on a wide variety of television programmes. Her particular specialities are hosting audience discussion and debate programmes, conducting celebrity interviews and presenting and writing in-depth documentaries.

☆

Born in Dunfermline, **Iain Banks** is one of the most acclaimed novelists in Scotland. Among his books are The Wasp Factory, *The Bridge* and *Crow Road*. He lives in North Queensferry, overlooking the Forth Rail Bridge.

☆

Born in Port Seton in 1942, **John Bellany** trained at Edinburgh College of Art and the Royal College of Art, London. He has received numerous awards and has exhibited in Boston, Dublin, New York and Warsaw. He was elected a member of the Royal Academy in 1991.

☆

Jackie Bird is one of the best-known faces in television in Scotland. She presents BBC Scotland's flagship nightly news programme *Reporting Scotland* as well as being host of other yearly BBC Scotland programmes such as the *Hogmanay Show* and *BBC Children In Need*.

☆

Dame Elizabeth Blackadder is one of Britain's most respected contemporary artists, producing floral, still-life and landscape paintings. She was the first woman elected to both the Royal Scottish Academy (1972) and the Royal Academy of Arts (1976).

☆

As an international yachtsman, **Sir Chay Blyth** has had a distinguished and adventure-filled life. In 1971, aboard the 59ft ketch *British Steel*, he became the first person to sail non-stop around the world against the prevailing winds and currents.

☆

Craig Brown had an outstanding record as manager of the Scotland football team, losing only nine competitive matches. In his playing days, he played for Rangers, Dundee and Falkirk.

☆

Along with Roy Williamson, **Ronnie Browne** was a member of the hugely popular folk duo, the Corries. The song that they will always be associated with is Roy's 'Flower of Scotland', the country's unofficial national anthem.

☆

Ken Bruce is one of Radio 2's stable of extremely popular presenters. His easy style attracts a huge listening audience every weekday.

☆

Edinburgh-born **Ronnie Corbett** is particularly noted for his highly successful and much-loved television comedy series, *The Two Ronnies*, with Ronnie Barker, a partnership which lasted for many years.

☆

As well as being Director of Nations and Regions for Channel 4, with overall responsibility for the channel's strategy outside London, **Stuart Cosgrove** presents the extremely popular *Off The Ball* for Radio Scotland with Tam Cowan.

☆

James Cosmo is one of Scotland's most respected actors and producers. He has played significant roles in such diverse films as *Braveheart* and *Trainspotting*, as well as in the successful television series *Roughnecks* about the oil industry.

☆

Alongside Stuart Cosgrove, **Tam Cowan** presents the award-winning radio show *Off the Ball* on Radio Scotland on Saturday afternoons, as well as the irreverent and highly popular series *Offside* for BBC Scotland, reflecting on the vagaries of Scottish football.

☆

Born in Dundee in 1946, **Brian Cox** is a highly experienced, respected and versatile actor on stage and screen. His film roles include Trotsky in *Nicholas and Alexandra*, Killearn in *Rob Roy* and Argyle Wallace in *Braveheart*.

☆

Bob Crampsey was born in Glasgow in 1930 and has had a distinguished career as a sports historian, analyst and commentator on radio, television and newspapers.

☆

As a producer, composer and performer of traditional and contemporary Celtic music, **Phil Cunningham** is one of Scotland's most respected and entertaining musicians.

☆

Recently retired, **Hugh Dallas** is Scotland's most respected international football referee. He has officiated in World Cups as well as European Championships, European club competitions and some of the most high-profile Scottish domestic matches of the past fifteen years.

☆

As an artist himself and promoter of artists, **Richard Demarco** has played an important part in shaping the art world in Scotland. He continues to encourage and inspire artists and photographers, including myself, with his unbridled and visionary enthusiasm.

☆

Based in Fife, **Isla Dewar** has written many successful novels, including the best-selling *Women Talking Dirty* which was made into a film starring Gina McKee and Helena Bonham Carter.

☆

Barbara Dickson is an actress and singer from Dunfermline. She has six platinum albums, eleven gold and seven silver. Her single, 'I Know Him So Well' (with Elaine Paige) sold a million copies.

☆

Dougie Donnelly is one of the BBC's top television sports presenters with more than twenty years experience of live broadcasting from the country's major sporting occasions. He is currently Chairman of the Scottish Institute of Sport.

☆

Gavin Esler joined the BBC *Newsnight* presenting team in January 2003. He has anchored BBC News 24 since 1997 and reported for news and documentary programmes across Europe, Russia, China and North and South America.

☆

Dr Winnie Ewing is the former President of the Scottish National Party. Her political life has been eventful and distinguished, earning respect from all parties in the UK and Europe, where she became known as Madame Écosse.

☆

Born in Govan, **Sir Alex Ferguson** started playing football at senior level with Queen's Park. He went on to play for St Johnstone, Dunfermline, Rangers, Falkirk and Ayr United. He has been manager of Manchester United since 1986 and was awarded a knighthood in 1999.

☆

Actor **Gregor Fisher** was born in Stirlingshire. His credits include *The Tales of Para Handy*, *The Railway Children*, *Nicholas Nickleby*, *Naked Video*, *Scotch and Wry* and the hugely successful *Rab C. Nesbitt*.

☆

Steve Forbes is a grandson of pioneering publisher Bertie Forbes, founder of the influential *Forbes* magazine. Based in New York and with Steve as President, *Forbes* is regarded as the leading business publication in its field.

☆

Rikki Fulton (1924-2004) was one of Scotland's best-loved comedians and actors. His annual Hogmanay appearance on *Scotch and Wry* became an institution. His films include *Gorky Park*, *Local Hero* and *Comfort and Joy*. In 1993, he received a Lifetime Achievement Award from BAFTA.

☆

Born in Aberdeen, **Evelyn Glennie** was the first full-time solo classical percussionist in the world. She has written and performed music for television, radio and film. In live performances she employs up to 60 instruments, *giving over 100* concerts a year.

☆

Born in Edinburgh and trained at the Royal Scottish Academy of Dramatic Art in Glasgow, **Hannah Gordon** is best remembered for her television appearances which include *Upstairs, Downstairs* and *My Wife Next Door*.

☆

Following an illustrious career as captain of Glasgow Rangers and Scotland, **John Greig** was voted Rangers' greatest ever player. He is now a director at Ibrox.

☆

After an outstanding career as captain of Liverpool FC, **Alan Hansen** has gone on to a highly successful media career as a football analyst with the BBC and presenter of excellent football documentaries.

☆

Buff Hardie is an Aberdonian, and was one third of the comedy revue *Scotland the What?*, which, from a home base of His Majesty's Theatre in Aberdeen, travelled regularly and successfully to all the major Scottish theatres *and beyond*.

☆

Born in Edinburgh in 1962, **Gavin Hastings**' rugby achievements include playing in three Rugby World Cups as well as featuring in Scotland's historic Grand Slam side of 1990. He was captain of the British Lions in New Zealand in 1993 and also captained Scotland on 20 occasions.

☆

Sarah Heaney is a freelance television presenter based in London. She recently fronted a new prime-time crime programme, *Manhunt—Solving Britain's Crimes*. Previously she was a presenter on STV's *Scotland Today* as well as travel and film programmes.

☆

Born in 1969 in Edinburgh, **Stephen Hendry** has achieved an unparalleled seven world titles in snooker. He was voted BBC Scotland's Sports Personality of the Year in 1987 and 1990, and in 1994 he was awarded an MBE.

☆

An entrepreneur and philanthropist, **Sir Tom Hunter**'s success in the world of business has benefited, through his generous donations, many diverse charitable causes throughout the world.

☆

Hazel Irvine joined BBC TV in 1990 as presenter of *Friday Sportscene* and has gone on to cover major events such as the Summer and Winter Olympics, the World Cup Finals and the Commonwealth Games. She is now a regular broadcaster for BBC Sport and BBC News.

☆

Based in the United States, **Alastair Johnston** is President of IMG International as well as being a director of Glasgow Rangers Football Club.

☆

Jimmy Johnstone (1944-2006) was Celtic's greatest ever footballer. Throughout his career, he tormented defences all over the world, at the same time gaining the respect, admiration and affection of teammates and opponents alike. His proudest moment was winning the European Cup against Inter Milan in Lisbon in 1967.

☆

Born in Lewis in the Outer Hebrides, **Calum Kennedy** (1928-2006) won the National Mod Gold Medal in 1955. He travelled the world performing in concerts and on television, captivating audiences with his wonderful singing voice.

☆

Daughter of Calum, **Fiona Kennedy** shares his beautiful singing voice in her treatment of both traditional and contemporary songs. She combines recording and performing with a career as a presenter and director of Tartan TV.

☆

Journalist, broadcaster and author, **Sir Ludovic Kennedy** was born in Edinburgh in 1919. On television he hosted *This Week*, contributed to BBC's *Panorama* and presented the television review programme, *Did You See?* His books include *Ten Rillington Place* and *A Presumption of Innocence*.

☆

In 2004, **Denis Law** was voted Scotland's greatest ever footballer, having starred for Manchester United and Scotland in the sixties and seventies.

☆

Denis Lawson has worked extensively on stage, film and television, most notably in Bill Forsyth's *Local Hero*. His stage work has also included award-winning musical performances in *Pal Joey* and *Mr Cinders*.

☆

Jim Leishman was born in Lochgelly, Fife in 1953. He enjoyed a very successful career with Dunfermline Athletic both as a player and, later, as a manager. He is currently director of football at the club.

☆

Jimmy Logan (1928-2001) was one of Scotland's best-loved entertainers. His first acting role was in 1949 in *Floodtide*, a drama set in Clydeside. Other theatrical successes included *The Entertainer* and *The Comedians*, as well as a remarkable performance in *Death of a Salesman* at the Pitlochry Festival Theatre.

☆

Kenny Logan has had a distinguished career in club and international rugby, having played for Stirling County, London Wasps, Glasgow and the Barbarians. Kenny has 70 international caps for Scotland.

☆

Born in Perthshire, **Fred MacAulay** began his full-time career in comedy at the age of 31, making a dramatic move from his former occupation as an accountant. Fred has hosted BBC Scotland's radio breakfast show since 1997.

☆

Alexander McCall Smith is one of Scotland's most prolific and successful novelists of recent times, particularly with his series based on the adventures of Precious Ramotswe, Botswana's only female private detective.

☆

Eileen McCallum was born in Glasgow, where she attended university and the Royal Scottish Academy of Dramatic Art. She has worked in television, theatre and film since the 1950s. She is now a regular member of the cast of *River City*.

☆

Born in Bellshill in North Lanarkshire in 1962, **Ally McCoist** is one of the greatest goal scorers of his generation. He was a key member of the Glasgow Rangers team that won nine League Championships in a row beginning in 1988/9. He has been capped 61 times for Scotland. He is currently Assistant Manager to Walter Smith at Rangers.

☆

Born in Glasgow, **Malky McCormick** is Scotland's best-known cartoonist. He is possibly best remembered for the hugely successful cartoon strip *The Big Yin*, which he devised with Billy Connolly.

☆

Originally from North Uist, **Calum Macdonald** is a founder member of the internationally acclaimed band Runrig. As well as being a percussionist, Calum's songwriting with his brother Rory conveys the essence of contemporary Gaelic culture.

☆

Ewan MacGregor was born in Crieff in Perthshire. He came to film prominence in *Shallow Grave* in 1994 and with the Oscar-nominated *Trainspotting* in 1996. He has played Obi Wan Kenobi in three Star Wars movies. His other films include *Moulin Rouge* and *Young Adam*.

☆

Musician and broadcaster **Jimmie Macgregor** was influential in the early days of the folk revival in Britain. He has written a number of books based on his long-distance walks programmes for radio and television and has twice been named Scot of the Year.

☆

Hugh McIlvanney is widely regarded as the outstanding sports writer of his generation. In 1996, he was awarded the OBE, and in 2004, the Scottish Daily Newspaper Society presented Hugh with a lifetime achievement award.

☆

Best known for his character of Archie in *Monarch of the Glen*, the extremely popular BBC series set near Newtonmore, **Alastair Mackenzie** has played many contrasting television roles in a wide variety of genres.

☆

Sir Cameron Mackintosh is a musical producer with an extensive list of successes behind him, including *Song and Dance*, *Les Misérables*, *Phantom of the Opera* and *Miss Saigon*. He was knighted in 1996 for his services to the British Theatre.

☆

Lorraine McIntosh enjoyed a very successful musical career with Deacon Blue alongside husband Ricky Ross, before becoming a regular actress on BBC's popular series, *River City*.

☆

Kenneth McKellar is one of Scotland's best-loved singers. In a long career he has entertained Scots at home and abroad with his classically trained voice. He is particularly well known for his distinctive recordings of the songs of Robert Burns.

☆

Kevin McKidd is one of Scotland's most versatile and respected actors both in the UK and, increasingly, abroad. His most recent starring role is in *Rome*, an epic saga set during the last years of Julius Caesar's reign.

☆

Born in Perthshire in 1954, **Dougie MacLean**'s early musical years were spent touring all over the UK and Europe as a member of the Tannahill Weavers, playing fiddle and sharing vocals. Dougie has since built an international reputation as a songwriter, composer and performer.

☆

Footballer **Billy McNeill** was born in 1940 in Bellshill, Lanarkshire. His most prolific days at centre-half and captain were at Celtic under Jock Stein. In May 1967 Billy became the first British footballer to hold aloft the European Cup after defeating Inter Milan in Lisbon.

☆

Journalist and mountaineer **Cameron McNeish** is one of Britain's best-known outdoor commentators. He is President of the Ramblers' Association in Scotland and has written several books including *Scotland's 100 Best Walks* and *The Wilderness World of Cameron McNeish*.

☆

Born in Glasgow, **Sally Magnusson** began her journalistic career on the *Scotsman* and went on to become one of the BBC's leading news presenters. Sally has won both newspaper and television awards including a Scottish BAFTA for *Dunblane Remembered*.

☆

Michael Marra was born in Lochee, Dundee in 1952. He is one of Scotland's most talented original songwriters and performers. In 1971 he formed his first band, Hen's Teeth, whose line-up included Dougie MacLean.

☆

Karen Matheson is often regarded as having the most beautiful traditional singing voice in Scotland today. As well as having a successful solo career, she is the principal singer of Capercaillie.

☆

Voted as Aberdeen FC's greatest ever player, **Willie Miller** captained the Dons to their most famous triumph in Gothenburg in 1983, when he held aloft the European Cup-Winners' Cup after defeating the famous Real Madrid. He is now Director of Football at Pittodrie.

☆

As an entrepreneur with an innovative approach to marketing, **Michelle Mone** has gained remarkable success with her company Ultimo. From modest beginnings, she has created a company of international significance through hard work and determination.

☆

Colin Montgomerie is Scotland's most successful international golfer. He has consistently ranked amongst the world's best golfers since moving into the top 10 of the World Rankings in 1994.

☆

Also known as Jolomo, **John Lowrie Morrison** is one of Scotland's most successful landscape painters, specialising in vibrant and evocative representations of Scotland's west coast and, more recently, Buchan. He has a studio in Tayvallich.

☆

Donnie Munro was born on the Isle of Skye. He has enjoyed much success as a singer/songwriter with Runrig and, more recently, in a solo capacity.

☆

Author, broadcaster and chef, **Nick Nairn** runs the very successful Nairn's Cook School on Lake of Menteith *in Stirlingshire*. He has filmed three successful television series with the BBC and appears regularly on programmes such as *Ready, Steady, Cook*, *Food and Drink* and *Landward*.

☆

Daniela Nardini was born and brought up in Largs. In a very successful career in theatre, television and film, Daniela has shown great versatility, from playing the main role of Mary in Liz Lochhead's *Mary Queen of Scots Got Her Head Chopped Off*, to the central character of Anna in *This Life* for BBC2.

☆

Bill Paterson was born in Glasgow, where he made his first professional appearance with the Citizens' Theatre in 1967. He has made many appearances at the National Theatre, the Royal Court and in the West End and has also worked extensively in film and television.

☆

Comedienne and raconteuse, **Dorothy Paul** was born in Dennistoun in Glasgow. She has a career-long history of playing pantomime before continuing into variety with other Scottish comedy stars such as the late Jack Milroy and Johnny Beattie.

☆

Marti Pellow is the lead singer of Wet, Wet, Wet, one of the most successful Scottish bands of the past twenty years.

☆

Colin Prior is an inspirational landscape photographer. Having produced beautiful books, calendars, prints and cards of Scotland's wilderness and wild places, he is now focusing his attention on the wild places of the world.

☆

Gerry Rafferty was a hugely successful musician at the end of the 1970s thanks, in part, to the still popular song 'Baker Street' and his solo album *City to City*, alongside memorable songs from his time with Stealer's Wheel. Gerry continues to write and record in his own distinctive style.

☆

Born in Cardenden in Fife in 1960, **Ian Rankin** is one of the most successful writers of the crime genre. In 2005 Ian was awarded the Crime Writers' Association's Diamond Dagger Award in recognition of his body of work to date.

☆

Eddi Reader was born and brought up in Glasgow. Starting as a backing singer for The Eurythmics and Alison Moyet, she came to the attention of a wide audience as the singer with Fairground Attraction. Since then she has produced many successful solo albums including the highly acclaimed *Songs of Robert Burns.*

☆

Siobhan Redmond is one of Scotland's most established actresses, having had many successes on stage, on television and on radio including the highly successful series *Between the Lines* and *Holby City* as well as varied roles in *Sea of Souls* and the acclaimed *The Smoking Room*.

☆

Lord George Robertson of Port Ellen is one of the UK's most respected politicians. He is a former NATO Secretary-General, serving from 1999 to 2003. Previously, he was Britain's Defence Secretary from 1997 to 1999.

☆

As a writer and actor, **Tony Roper**'s career has been rich and varied. *One of his* finest achievements has been the enormous success of *The Steamie*, a fascinating and hugely entertaining insight into Glasgow's social history set in a communal laundry.

☆

Sister of Jimmy Logan, **Annie Ross** has spent most of her life in the United States pursuing a highly successful career as a jazz singer.

☆

Originally from Dundee, **Ricky Ross** has followed his hugely successful career with Deacon Blue by establishing himself as a respected songwriter and solo performer.

☆

As a journalist, writer and television reporter based in Brussels, **Angus Roxburgh** has been one of the leading commentators on European events in recent years, both as BBC's European correspondent and, more recently, as a freelance journalist.

☆

Dougray Scott is one of Scotland's most accomplished and versatile film, television and theatrical actors. His films include *Mission Impossible 2*, *Enigma*, *Ripley's Game* and *To Kill a King*.

☆

After beginning his working life in the shipyards, **Alan Sharp** has had a prolific and successful career as a screenwriter for film and television. His writing has received much acclaim, in particular his screenplay for *Rob Roy* in 1995.

☆

Glasgow-born **Carol Smillie** began her career as a model. More recently she has worked as a television presenter, notably on *Changing Rooms*, one of the first home improvement shows.

☆

Gordon Smith was appointed Chief Executive of the Scottish Football Association in June 2007. He was a professional player for seventeen years with, among others, Rangers and Manchester City. Before taking up his SFA post, he was an excellent football analyst on BBC Scotland.

☆

Leader of the Liberal Party from 1976 to 1988, **Sir David Steel** was knighted in 1990. In 1999, Sir David, or Lord Steel of Aikwood, became the first Presiding Officer of the new Scottish Parliament, standing down in 2003.

☆

Dawn Steele is best known for her role as Lexie in the highly successful BBC series *Monarch of the Glen*, set in the Scottish Highlands, which she played for five years. Among other projects, she has starred in *Sea of Souls* with one of Scotland's most respected actors, Bill Paterson.

☆

Appointed manager of Celtic in 2005, **Gordon Strachan** has had an extremely successful playing career at club and international level. As well as being a Premiership manager with Southampton, he has enjoyed much success as a football analyst with the BBC.

☆

An academic, originally from Airth, **Dr Tom Sutherland** moved to the United States early in his career. In 1985, two years after taking up a position of Dean of Faculty in the American University of Beirut in Lebanon, Tom was kidnapped by gunmen from the Islamic Jihad. He spent nearly six and a half years in captivity.

☆

Emma Thompson is one of Britain's most accomplished actresses and has received Oscars in 1992 for best actress in *Howard's End* and in 1995 for the best screenplay with *Sense and Sensibility*.

☆

Sam Torrance was born in Largs in Ayrshire. He became a professional golfer in 1970 and has enjoyed significant success. Of his Ryder Cup matches, his win at the Belfry in 1985 is his most memorable.

☆

Kirsty Wark was born in Dumfries and is one of Scotland's most respected television presenters. She joined BBC2's current affairs programme *Newsnight* in 1993. In 1997 she won the BAFTA Scotland Best Television Presenter Award.

☆

Born in Glasgow, actor **Jonathan Watson** trained at the Royal Scottish Academy of Music and Drama. His involvement with BBC Scotland's Comedy Unit first brought him to the public's attention, and he is best known for his satirical look at Scottish football, *Only an Excuse?*

☆

Journalist and broadcaster **Jack Webster** was born in 1931 in the village of Maud, Aberdeenshire. Jack has written fourteen books, including his evocative autobiography *Grains of Truth* and the history of his beloved Aberdeen Football Club.

☆

Louise White is a presenter on STV's flagship news programme *Scotland Today*, having begun her career on Radio Scotland.

☆

Richard Wilson was born in Greenock and trained at the Royal Academy of Dramatic Art in London. He is particularly loved for his award-winning portrayal of the irascible character Victor Meldrew in the television series *One Foot in the Grave*. In 1994, Richard was awarded an OBE for services to drama as a director and actor.

☆

Sir Ian Wood is Chairman and Chief Executive of the Wood Group, one of the leading companies in the global oil industry, based in Aberdeen.

☆

Kirsty Young is one of the country's top newscasters. She was born in Glasgow in 1968 and began her journalistic career in 1989 as a newsreader for Radio Scotland. She has since been a presenter on STV, BBC, ITV and Channel 5 and currently hosts *Desert Island Discs* on Radio 4.

☆